SMALL CHURCH, BIG VISION

SMALL CHURCH, BIG VISION

How your church can change the world

Marshall Pickering
An Imprint of HarperCollins*Publishers*

Marshall Pickering is an Imprint of
HarperCollins*Religious*
Part of HarperCollins*Publishers*
77–85 Fulham Palace Road, London W6 8JB

First published in Great Britain
in 1995 by Marshall Pickering

A catalogue record for this book is
available from the British Library

ISBN 0 551 02904–8

Typeset by Harper Phototypesetters Limited
Northampton, England
Printed and bound in Great Britain by
HarperCollinsManufacturing Glasgow

CONTENTS

PART 4 GETTING IT TOGETHER

INTRODUCTION

Two thousand years ago Jesus commissioned his disciples to 'make disciples of all the nations, teaching them to observe all that I have taught you'. Establishing churches was fundamental to their understanding of how they should do this, and establishing a church was the first thing they did wherever they went. The local church is a crucial part of the discipling of a town, region or nation and is consequential to the completion of the Great Commission given by Jesus.

For a small church in an inauspicious location, getting hold of a vision for their contribution to the job of World Mission can be difficult at best. Yet without this understanding, no church, however big, can be fully fulfilling its destiny.

With the exception of a handful of churches, the huge majority of the world's four million churches hold one thing in common: almost every church on earth is or has been a small church. Today the majority of the world's churches have less than 120 regular attenders. In England, 40 per cent of all churches have less than fifty adults at all Sunday services, and for more than one in ten churches there are fewer than twenty-five attenders.

Of course there are different strengths and limitations in a church of twenty-five than there are in a church of eighty. But research has shown that churches of less than 120 share many of the same dynamics, as they are of a size where every member can have some knowledge of every other member. It is this common knowledge and relationship which in effect defines the local church and it is with these congregations in mind that this book has been written.

Being small is not in itself either a good thing or a bad thing. What is more important is the attitude of a small church to its role in the big vision of mission. In a recent survey it was found that the leaders of only a third of Protestant churches in Britain had a strong sense that the primary function of their church was to share the good news. Less than a quarter had a structured programme of evangelism in their church. With the job of world mission being so tied to the local church and with so many of them being small, it is important that the dynamics, strengths and role of the smaller local congregation are understood in terms of the Great Commission, not just by small church leaders, but by the leaders of big churches as well, who need consciously to create the natural strengths of the smaller congregation in their churches, and by all who are interested in world evangelization.

As authors we confess to a passion for world mission. One of us comes from a local church which started with fourteen members and now has congregations on three continents, the other comes from a missions agency that helps to resource and plant missionary churches. To our pleasure we have seen a shift in attitude by missionary organizations towards recognizing the importance of the local church in mission and a growing sense of responsibility for missions by a number of significant local churches. It is our desire to see this process continue and accelerate, and to this end we offer our thoughts in this book on the developing of a mission's mentality and programme in the average local congregation.

Back in 1966, a group of evangelical leaders met in

Berlin and committed themselves to reaching the world in one generation. By the usual understandings of a generation, we must be approaching that deadline. In the same vein, many missions organizations have taken the year AD 2000 as a pragmatic target to achieve certain mission objectives. As a result, as we approach the end of this millennium and the beginning of the next, local churches are faced with unprecedented opportunities for involvement in missions and the psychological benefit of a new era. Will the Church be a new community for the new millennium or an old institution from the past? The issue could hinge on whether churches are looking inwards to preserve what they have or looking outwards to pioneer new things for the Lord. It is the difference between a primarily pastoral church and a missionary church.

The world need millions of missionary congregations if the Bible's vision of people from every tribe, tongue and place worshipping the Lord is ever to be fulfilled. It is our hope that this book will inspire the vision and confidence needed for many churches to take a more active role in completing the Great Commission.

Lynn Green and Chris Forster
August 1994

PART ONE

SMALL CHURCH

WHAT IS THE SMALL CHURCH?

> And gathering them together, he commanded them not to leave Jerusalem, but to wait for what the Father had promised . . . He said to them 'you shall receive power when the Holy Spirit has come upon you; and you shall be my witnesses both in Jerusalem and in all Judea and Samaria and even to the remotest part of the Earth'. Acts 1:4–8

Jesus planted the first church in Jerusalem. It was he whose ministry had first 'converted' the founding members. It was he who gathered them together in Galilee after his resurrection, (Matt 28:7) and it was he who instructed them to leave their homes and set up a new base a hundred miles away in Jerusalem.

Some critics have postulated that Jesus had no intention of founding the church, but despite what they have said, we believe that Jesus did specifically and deliberately found a church and, according to his commissioning brief, it was to have two purposes: first, to be the receptacle of the Holy Spirit (Acts 1:5), the mediated presence of God on earth, the continuing 'body of Christ'; and second, to make Jesus known locally, nationally and universally (Acts 1:8). These two aspects of the church's *raison d'être* are in fact complementary parts of a bigger plan, which we shall examine in greater depth later in this book.

SMALL CHURCH, BIG VISION

Jesus' three or four years of ministry had touched thousands of people, changed the course of history, sown the seeds of renewal in spiritual and earthly kingdoms and reconciled the Creator with his wayward creation. However, in tangible terms, Jesus had simply planted a relatively small church and left it an enormous job to do.

The believing church has primarily been made up of congregations small enough to meet in a house. In the immediate aftermath of the Day of Pentecost, we still find the expanded Jerusalem church enjoying fellowship in private homes, although they were also meeting for larger 'celebrations' in the temple. This important relationship between the local church and the wider church will be explored in more detail later on. Prayer meetings were held in homes (Acts 12:12), and as the gospel spread we find Paul writing to churches meeting in homes (Col 4:15, Philem 2, Rom 16:5).

As the Church began, so it continued. Statistics gathered by Patrick Johnston, author of *Operation World*, show that world-wide the average local church has about 145 regular attenders. However, the statistics are skewed somewhat by the recent emergence of huge churches like the Yoido Full Gospel Church in Seoul, South Korea, which has nearly 750,000 members, so the vast majority of the world's churches are smaller than this average figure. In the USA, the average church size has been around seventy-five adults for some time. In Latin America, where overall church growth is extremely fast, the average still is only eighty-eight. Africa and India have higher averages closer to 150, but Europe and the rest of the West are predominantly lower. Research carried out in Germany by DAWN Europa in 1993 found the average size of a Protestant congregation to be only forty-four people. Most of these figures don't include children; if they did the figures would of course be a little higher. The 1989 English Church Census showed an average attendance of 128 including children for all churches and 111 when considering only evangelical churches. If we count adults only, these figures are reduced to ninety-six and seventy-eight respectively.

We must also remember that in all churches there are normally more regulars missing on any one Sunday than there are visitors. All things considered, it is tempting to speculate that the typical world church has about 120 regular member of all ages. In other words, it is of similar size to the original Upper Room Congregation of the Jerusalem church on the day of Pentecost.

However, the 1989 English Church Census also showed that over a third of Protestant churches have less than fifty adult attenders and nearly two thirds weighed in at less than 100. If we add to these the fact that over 1000 new churches have been planted since the census (according to an informal poll of denominational figures), then we can safely assume that there are over 15,000 small churches in England.

Elsewhere, in countries like Saudi Arabia or China, Christians meet in small groups because larger meetings are vulnerable to secular and religious authorities. In many places, economic and social factors mean that larger buildings are not available, so individual congregations must remain small. If the church of Jesus Christ is ever going to complete the Great Commission, then the small church must understand its role. If the Church in England and the rest of Europe is to start growing again, then the small church must learn to play its part to the full, and not leave mission to the handful of larger congregations.

At this point, it is important to give a working definition of the 'small church', though we shall need to unpack it and justify it later on.

In a paper entitled 'Unique Dynamics of a Small Church', the American researcher Carl Dudley states that small churches are single-cell churches. By this he means that all members of the church are expected to have some form of relationship with all other members. The specific relationship doesn't have to be deep and wide ranging, but it should encompass everyone. Research in the USA indicates that this type of structure reaches its limits between 150 and 200 people in a single congregation. In Europe the limit seems to be somewhat lower. The 1989 English Church Census showed that the fastest growing section of the Church is to be found in congregations of 100 to 150 adults.

Numbers aside, this cellular understanding of the small church gives us a useful key for defining the small church to which this book is addressed. The small church is the coming together of Christians within a geographical location or sociological sector for the purpose of expressing their life in Jesus more fully. These groups are limited in size because of our inability to have intimate relationships with large groups of people, and they are therefore unlikely to exceed 130 people; in the majority of situations they will be considerably smaller.

Because the word 'cell' is more normally used to describe a slightly different aspect of church life than that described above, we shall most often use the term 'congregation' (or sometimes 'local church') to describe the expression of the church for which this book has been written.

Many of you may now be wondering whether this book has any relevance to you at all, particularly if we are going to be concentrating on churches that are around 130-strong. But don't be deterred. We intend to examine the way in which local congregations fit into God's plan for the world at all levels, and how they can make their most vital contribution to the big vision that is often called 'The Great Commission'. Whether it's two or three gathered in his name, people meeting in someone's home, meeting in a back street hall or 100 in a town centre, all of these local and small expressions of the church have an important role to play in making Christ known in their neighbourhood and in all the world.

To illustrate just how effective a small church can be, we shall be examining some developments at Henley-on-Thames Baptist Church, a local congregation of fewer than 100 people in a small, largely affluent town in the South of England. As you will see, this church provides a powerful example of how a relatively small congregation can play a disproportionately large role in fulfilling the Great Commission.

The church building is on Henley High Street and provides a small bookshop and a coffee bar called Day Spring, which is open every shopping day, providing a regular interface with townsfolk. In spite of this and other commitments to outreach, the minister, Frank Payne, has experienced a measure of frustration due to the fact that the church cannot seem to grow beyond 100. If all the people who have attended regularly during the last three years were to turn up on a Sunday, they would probably double the size of the congregation. But, as with so many churches these days, people seem to attend for a while and then move somewhere else.

A couple of years ago, Frank attended a seminar sponsored by the Baptist Church on discipleship, where he met Misha Grigoriyan, a Baptist leader from Kazakhstan. Frank and Misha took a liking to one another almost immediately. As a result, Misha extended his trip so he could spend an extra week with Frank and the people of Henley Baptist.

Friendship between Church leaders is all too rare in the former Soviet Union, but in Frank and his fellow leaders at Henley Baptist, Misha was able to observe a style of leadership which valued genuine, deep relationships. Henley Baptist Church have maintained a good standing within the Baptist Union, and have also fully identified with one of the networks of newer churches.

For a week, Misha entered into the life of Henley Baptist and was drawn to what he saw. But it wasn't just a one-way relationship. Frank also began to absorb Misha's burden for his country. He had recently attended the first DAWN ('Disciplining A Whole Nation') Congress and had begun 'to get a vision for the nations'. This budding friendship with a leader from Kazakhstan provided a possible outlet for the vision.

What Misha Grigoriyan saw at Henley Baptist was a revelation to him. The Baptist Church in his home city of Shymkent is more than 100-strong, but it still carries the scars from the years of oppression. Like so many of the evangelical or Pentecostal churches of the former USSR, it has a legalistic flavour. And although the congregation is committed, there is little effort to take the life of the church into the community.

Henley Baptist had made the most of its High Street position by developing its bookshop and coffee bar. Misha was inspired by this commitment to outreach and he loved the freedom of worship. He was also impressed by the regular morning prayer meeting, where many of the members of the congregation gather to start the day in prayer.

Misha decided to invite Frank to visit his church in Shymkent with the expectation that new ideas and a fresh vision would revive the church. Frank accepted the invitation along with two other members of the congregation:

Malcolm, the church administrator, who felt he might be able to help set up a coffee bar and bookshop, and Maurice, a businessman who was in the process of becoming a Christian. Maurice was not the sort of man who would happily settle into a house group and Frank saw an opportunity to get closer to him on the trip so he could help him along the road of commitment to Christ.

Kazhakstan is one of the largest republics of the former Soviet Union. It is as big as all of Western Europe, but has a population of only seventeen million. About two million people live in the south-western region, which is called Shymkent. Though we in the West rarely hear anything about Kazakhstan, it is a significant country: it is rich in oil and other natural resources, but it also has potential for ethnic strife. Kazhaks make up about 60 per cent of the population, with Russians, Uzbecs, and other ethnic groups making up the balance. Given the potential for ethnic strife, the government has set up a charitable agency, Juskazinterethnos, whose task it is to develop ethnic harmony. It is through this agency that Henley Baptist Church is now working.

In Shymkent, the three men from Henley Baptist were faced with a variety of needs, opportunities and invitations to help. As they travelled around the city and the large surrounding region, Misha revealed an exceptional network of contacts amongst government officials. As Malcolm and Maurice investigated different business opportunities, Frank arranged for a delegation of English teachers from Kazakh schools to visit Henley-on-Thames. But the Shymkent authorities were also very keen to recruit English teachers from the UK to improve the standard of language teaching in the region. When the regional minister of education asked Frank to recruit teachers for the area, he felt he was getting in over his head. After all, how many English teachers could be found and spared from a congregation of fewer than 100 people?

On their return to Henley, the congregation was infected by the enthusiasm and vision of the three men and everyone got involved in preparations to receive the Kazakh teachers. This exercise provided a practical education about communicating with central Asia, getting visas, making travel arrangements, dealing in an unstable foreign currency, etc. In the end, 75 per cent of the congregation were involved, either as hosts to the teachers or as tour guides or drivers.

Only one of the eight teachers from Kazhakstan was a Christian. She had accepted Christ when Frank spoke at a meeting in Shymkent. But the others were fascinated with the church and the way these English people worshipped God, and all of them had probing questions about Jesus and what it means to be a Christian. They had suffered under an oppressive regime in Kazhakstan and several of them received individual counsel.

Not long after the teachers returned to Shymkent, Frank, Malcolm and Maurice visited again. With the successful visit of the English teachers behind them, the opportunities were even greater. Juskazinterethnos wanted to help with business and education so, during this second trip, plans were drawn up for an English Language and Business Centre.

Henley Baptist already had some links with Youth With A Mission as a result of sending one of their members to a YWAM team in Poland. At this point, YWAM were drawn in to provide much needed support. They were already involved in neighbouring Uzbekistan and were happy to extend into Shymkent. They were also happy to work under the auspices of the Equip Trust which Henley Baptist had set up for the work in Kazhakstan.

This contact with a mission agency provided much

needed support, further expertise and access to greater resources. The next step was for Frank to take some of the YWAM leaders to Kazhakstan and introduce them to the key government and church leaders he had already met. From the YWAM point of view, this first trip confirmed that Frank's leadership and pastoral input was vital to the success of the project.

Frank and his co-workers at Henley Baptist took a relational approach to this project – they called for help from those they knew and trusted. Through the network of new churches, several other congregations have heard about the opportunities in Shymkent and are planning some sort of involvement. The Baptist Union connection has opened many doors in Kazakhstan and has strengthened fellowship within the international movement. The YWAM link has brought greater experience, people resources and a closer link with other mission efforts in central Asia.

As this book goes to press, all these different partners are operating under Equip Trust, which was established by Frank, Maurice and Malcolm. The regional authorities in Shymkent see the Equip Trust as a vital source of assistance for their people. Under it, English teachers are being recruited, trained and sent to teach in Shymkent colleges. An English reading library is being planned. A series of business training seminars is being conducted and architects are developing the plans for the English Language and Business Centre. YWAM is providing much of the teaching and many of the staff who will be required for the projects. Maurice is planning some business initiatives that will help the region in their efforts to develop private enterprise. Through the YWAM link, many other business people are involved, in the hope that their participation will lead to even more business links with Christian businessmen in Western countries.

This kind of project illustrates how, through a network of good relationships, a small congregation can make a big impact in foreign missions. The Shymkent project can be a model for an effective approach to missions. It demonstrates that a small congregation can be the catalyst for gathering and focusing the resources of other churches, a denomination and at least one mission agency. It also demonstrates that the Church can be found in many different kinds of organizational structures.

What has all of this meant for the life of Henley Baptist? We recently put that question to Frank. He replied, 'Over fifteen years I have been at this church, we have sought to establish a clear outreach philosophy. The Day Spring Centre has provided a place where many volunteers have got involved. It is a coffee shop, a bookshop and is a gathering point for mums and toddlers. It provided a great place for the Kazakh teachers to gather, have their meals and meet with church folk.

'We have also had some really special occasions as a result of overseas involvement. After Misha's wife committed her life to Christ, she wanted to be baptized, but she wanted me to do the service. It worked out for her to be here in England when the Kazakh teachers were visiting, so we had a special bilingual service and she was baptized. It was a great occasion for the whole congregation.

'None of the church folk seem to resent our involvement thus far. It is seen as the international extension of our outreach philosophy. However, it has stretched our ability to provide pastoral care locally. So we took the risk of calling a second minister. We thought we took a fairly unusual step, in that we did not call a younger man, but we called an older man who had demonstrated a clear pastoral gifting. This has strengthened our stability while I have become more and more involved with the ministry in

Shymkent. This step has stretched us beyond our normal financial limits, but we have felt that we should go ahead as a step of faith and so far, God has provided.'

Over the past few years, Frank's attitude to overseas mission has changed quite a lot. In his early years of ministry, if someone came to him reporting a calling to go abroad, his initial reaction was, 'What are you running from?' He continues, 'I could always see some pastoral need in their lives, something that needed improvement before they went anywhere.' It was also difficult for him and his people to see badly needed members leaving their home post.

He also expressed some of the pressures and reactions that many ministers feel when they are confronted with the activities of mission agencies. 'I now realize how much pressure I was under to see my congregation grow. If it didn't grow, I considered myself a failure. When people wanted to leave to join a mission agency, I felt it was a distraction from my main responsibility. I now realize that there was quite a competitive spirit in me.

'Then I was asked to speak at a YWAM Discipleship Training School in Amsterdam. When I got there and a big, tall YWAM leader showed me around all the activities and facilities, I couldn't help but think how well I could do in Henley if I could cream the best talent from all the churches and get them to pay their tithes up front! I was threatened and reacted badly. Just at that point this man, Floyd McClung, said, "Pastor Frank, I am about to go speak in a meeting. I really need God's anointing. Could you please pray for me?"

'That simple request challenged my attitude, and from that point, I began to be inspired with ideas of what we could do in my congregation. God gradually impressed upon me that the prime function of the local church is to be

13

an equipping and sending agency, but you have to be secure in your own calling. If God wants us to remain small and keep sending out more and more people, then that is fine with me.

'I also began to see that, not only should local church support mission, but mission should support local church. Mission agencies are called to support the local churches in their work to fulfil the Great Commission. If mission agencies could get alongside churches and encourage them in their calling, rather than employing guilt and overwhelming statistics, then we could always work in partnership, and the churches would be fully involved and would reap the benefits. In this project, relationships have been the key. Relationship with Misha, with YWAM, the Baptist Union and the network of new churches under Barney Coombs' leadership.'

We have taken the time and space to recount and analyse aspects of Henley Baptist's Kazakhstan project in some depth. It illustrates several of the strengths that are unique to smaller churches. Henley Baptist's size has meant that a majority of the congregation could be involved in the one project. It has been able to focus its energies and to be a very welcoming and personal environment for Kazakh visitors.

So, there are advantages to being small. There are also some very good reasons why a church should be small. But there are bad reasons too, and even some ugly ones.

2

WHY ARE CHURCHES SMALL?

Smallness is not a purely numerical phenomenon; it is also defined by intimacy in relationships. However, it is clear that even with this more qualitative definition of the small church there are many churches that do not fulfil their potential in numerical terms. These churches could be said to be small in two dimensions, and before they can fully engage in the big vision they need to address the reasons for their numerical weakness. Then they need either to come to terms with these reasons or to change them.

In the seminal missions classic *Understanding Church Growth*, Dr Donald McGavran observes that, while there is truth in the cliché 'numbers are unimportant', when it is related to the church, as soon as it becomes a general proposition it is without biblical basis. He writes, 'The revelation of God throughout history assumes that the numbers of the redeemed do count. It believes, for example, that as "grace extends to more and more people", thanksgiving to the glory of God increases' (2 Cor 4:15).

There are many reasons why churches are small, some good, some bad and some ugly; some biblical, others theological; some contextual, others cultural; and some strategic, others accidental or even sinful.

THE GOOD

One good reasons for being small is being new. The church in Ephesus is started by Paul's conversion of twelve of John the Baptist's disciples. Similarly today, new churches in new places will have to start small. Being new is obviously a good reason for being small, although if all big churches start small, then smallness can not be reason in itself for not growing.

Apart from being new, there are plenty of biblical reasons for smallness in church life. In Acts 2:42, we read a list of ongoing activities that characterized the life of the first church as it grew in Jerusalem: teaching, fellowship, breaking of bread and prayer. All of these activities have biblical precedents at both the intimate and the mass level.

Although Jesus taught the multitudes, much of the teaching was given to a smaller group of twelve or seventy disciples. When Jesus breaks bread with five thousand he does so by breaking them into groups of fifty to one hundred. The Greek word for these groups literally means 'drinking parties', so five thousand or more people had fellowship in these smaller groups. In Acts 2, we read that the whole Jerusalem church (i.e. more than 3000 people) was 'continuing with one mind in the temple'. This phrase is used of the church five times in the first five chapters of Acts and clearly refers to agreement in prayer (Acts 1:14, 2:1, 4:24). Acts 3:1 confirms that the disciples met at the temple to pray; however, in the context of his church, Jesus explicitly refers to two agreeing in prayer (Matt 18:19).

It is clear that there is a biblical mandate for church activity taking place in the more intimate context of the smaller group, while at the same time expressing a unity with other such small groups or churches in larger gatherings or celebrations. This unity of purpose at the wider level is fundamental to a small church being involved in a bigger vision. A church that is small because it has understood its part in God's bigger plan, is a church that is small for the right reasons.

One example is the 'Church in the Field' in Kedington, Suffolk, which has about thirty committed members, although Sunday attendance will sometimes reach as many as fifty people. The Church in the Field is small partly because it is new, but also because it has an understanding of its role in God's plan and this is likely to keep it small for some time to come.

Few of the many villages in the area have an active church, so the core members of the Church in the Field take their worship from village to village. They go to all the trouble of moving from place to place for two reasons: they feel that it is important to 'lift up the name of Jesus' in places where he has not been publicly worshipped for many decades, and they believe that God has spoken to them about 'rebuilding the ancient ruins'. Once there were many churches and chapels full of worshippers in these villages. They believe that God wants to re-establish a presence, and their worship is a start.

When greater growth comes, they don't anticipate that it will be in the form of an ever-larger single congregation in their home village. Rather, they expect to see new congregations in the many villages round about. Thirty to fifty people is about the right size to fit into the village halls and community centres that are dotted here and there, so they intend to reproduce the model God has given them rather than trying to develop bigger congregations.

The Church in the Field is small and is likely to remain small because of the way they understand their role in God's plan for the area. This plan influences their physical location and style of ministry in ways that require them to stay small. The implications of their physical location on their size helps highlight a set of related good reasons for being small. These could be referred to as strategic positioning.

As you read this, the Church of Jesus Christ is undergoing a phenomenal spurt of growth all over the world and on every continent. In many of these revival areas much of the increased church growth can be shown to relate to a new wave of strategic church planting. This process has come to be known as the DAWN strategy (DAWN is an acronym for 'Disciple A Whole Nation'.) The DAWN strategy seeks to mobilize the body of Christ in a process of ongoing strategic Church planting until every village, community, subculture, kind and class of people have a witnessing, Christ-centred congregation continually taking the gospel to them. The success of DAWN in nations as varied as Brazil, India, Rumania and New Zealand has many contributing factors, and two of these factors have particular relevance to the size of the churches in these places.

First, DAWN avoids the limits to growth of a single-cell local congregation – 'the 200 barrier' or 'the 150 barrier' – by continually challenging congregations that are approaching this level to plant a new congregation, effectively making room for further growth. A couple of years ago a pastor from Holland visited the original congregation of the Ichthus Christian Fellowship, a fast-growing group of congregations in south-east London. At the time he visited, the congregation was about 100. He commented on how small and uninspiring the church seemed compared with some other other well-known churches he had visited. He was right of course. However, very few of those other churches could say that their members had been responsible for planting over 30 churches in London, several in other parts of the country, two in Cyprus, two in Turkey (making it the biggest Evangelical denomination), two in Bulgaria, one in Albania, one in France and one in Azerbaijan. In seventeen years, the original Ichthus congregation had grown from fourteen people to about 100, but it was still quite small for very good reasons.

The challenge of the DAWN strategy, for growing churches to continually bless communities outside their immediate area, will limit the maximum size of the local congregation. The net results are invariably and demonstrably far greater than they would be if a church simply goes on increasing the target area of its single congregation.

The second size-limiting factor in the DAWN strategy relates to the determination to place new congregations so as to open up communities that were untouched by the work of the planting church or agency. These communities are often untouched because they are either small or particularly resistant to the gospel. Both reasons will place limits on the likely size of the new congregation.

A good example of the importance of strategic location was presented at a regional DAWN consultation in Norfolk. A minister shared how he worked in a village of 1500 people with two churches, an Anglican Church and a Methodist Church. The leaders from these two churches decided to work out where their members lived. When they did, they were surprised to find that neither church was reaching anybody from a new housing estate that had been added to the old village. This estate represented at least a third of the population. As a result, the Methodist Church started a second family service in a community hall on the estate. At the time of the consultation, thirty new people were attending the service.

This type of strategic positioning aimed at opening up a new community is biblical: Paul does it in Corinth, where after preaching to the Jews and God-fearing Gentiles and collecting a group of believers at the synagogue, he decided he is going to preach to the Gentiles. To do this he moves a few yards sideways into a Gentile school which he uses as his new base of operations.

Communities are best reached with the gospel in the natural course of their lives. If our churches are not located where people naturally spend their time, we will only reach those who are highly motivated to find God. A church strategically placed to reach a small community, whether it is a village, a housing estate or the Chinese population in Bournemouth, cannot expect to grow to the size of a town-centre counterpart. However, it may be able to create links with other local churches to experience the larger context of fellowship which the Jerusalem church enjoyed at the Temple. Similarly, small churches that are holding ground and maintaining a presence in resistant sections of our society should be honoured by the wider church and supported until such time as we see numerical break-throughs.

There are literally thousands of rural churches that are small purely because they are reaching a well-defined but small and diminishing population. The demographic changes of the last 150 years have left a huge number of small rural communities. The English Church Census showed that 45 per cent of all churches were in rural situations or commuter dormitories (29 per cent rural area, 16 per cent rural commuter dormitory). These two classifications of church environment were the only two to record an average congregation of less than 100 adults (thirty-seven and sixty-five respectively). Research by the Bible Society has shown that 62 per cent of rural churches have less than 50 adult attenders. Significantly, a greater than average number of rural churches had grown in the five years before the Church Census (42 per cent for rural and

33 per cent for rural commuter dormitory areas), the highest figures for any environment. It must be said that an above average number were declining as well. All of this indicates that, in a very changeable environment, a good proportion of these churches are doing a commendable job serving populations that are unlikely to be reached by churches outside their immediate area.

Before finishing our overview of good reasons for being small, a cautionary observation is called for. We started by arguing that all the activities of church can occur in a small group, and there is a biblical mandate for them to do so. Most successful large churches world-wide have recognized this and have structured themselves to provide this expression of church life in smaller congregations or cells. However, it is equally important that the small church, which provides this forum naturally, also finds a way to allow its members to take part in the wider expression of church life in the area or nation. The success of events like Spring Harvest and various Bible weeks is based on this important dynamic. Similarly, more and more small churches that are successful in joining in with the big vision of world mission are doing so by partnering with the wider body of Jesus in an area. There is no biblical precedent for the isolated, independent church whatever its size. This leads us naturally to look at some of the bad reasons why churches are small.

THE BAD

If there are good biblical, contextual and strategic reasons for being small, then there are related bad theological, cultural and accidental reasons as well.

In one sense, it is a shame to have to deal with bad

theological reasons for smallness so early in this book. If there is one thing likely to prompt a Christian leader to throw a book through the air in a pique of righteous anger and to leave it unread through eternity, it is categorizing a dearly held doctrine as a hindrance to the gospel. In fairness we must emphasize that we know of churches and individuals of most theological persuasions who actively and successfully evangelize, so we will deal with these issues in a broad and non-specific way to allow practically all readers to side-step any personal criticism. At the same time, we pray that the Holy Spirit will highlight any doctrines in the reader's church that may be used as an excuse for smallness.

Remnant Theology

Remnant Theology is a system of thought that maintains that there are very few real Christians. And it expects things to get worse and worse until Jesus can't bear to watch any more and comes for 'the few'. Once that is accepted, then evangelism becomes something that Christians do to be faithful, without much hope of success. When a Remnant theologian reads about God's broad inclusive plans, he explains that 'all might be saved' is just an anthropomorphic metaphor which really means five people get into heaven so long as they have a letter from their leading elder.

The position that we have painted is of course extreme, but the principals of Remnant Theology are at work in literally thousands of churches across Europe. They result in an exclusiveness that is reluctant to acknowledge 'outsiders' (people who do not regularly attend their group) as Christians. These principles also tend to reduce expectations for church growth and any sense of responsibility for mission.

Like all the best cons these ideas contain kernels of truth.

Jesus says that not everyone who calls him Lord really knows him. His parables are quite clear that not all will be saved and ultimately God must take responsibility for his fallen creation. However, these truths are not mutually exclusive with the ideas that *most* who call themselves Christian are, that in any place or time the *majority* of people can be Christians, and that *the church* also has a responsibility in God's redemptive plan.

Three consequences of Remnant Theology will keep churches smaller than they could be.

First, Remnant Theology will set up a false standard for determining spiritual maturity. By this standard, maturity is attained by conforming to a particular code of behaviour and certain distinctive doctrines. Over the years we have seen many new Christians fail to integrate into local churches when the validity of their salvation experience is belittled because they don't yet understand or agree with all the truths held in common by the local congregation. The excuse is often made by the church that they were obviously 'seed that fell on rocky ground'. But these Christians don't always lose faith, they just give up on church. Perhaps this is why three independent pieces of research have indicated the 60-80 per cent of the population in England would consider themselves Christians, yet our churches incorporate less than a quarter of them.

An evangelist we know once went to lead a mission. During his initial meeting with the congregation one man asked if he was 'going to preach the whole gospel'. When asked what the gentleman meant by this, he replied, 'abstinence from alcohol'. If any church is going to grow it needs to learn to recognize the work of the Holy Spirit in terms that do not simply reflect how well a person measures up to a set of theological propositions or behavioural dictates.

We can cite more than one incident where a congregation has been incensed by a new convert using an expletive to describe how good they feel about their conversion. And one church leader was involved in leading a homosexual to Christ and then praying that Jesus would change his sexual orientation; the new convert returned the next week proud that he had slept with a woman for the first time in his life. How would you have reacted?

We are not arguing that, if the church adopted a *laissez faire* attitude towards sin it would then grow. We firmly believe that the church needs to state the truth clearly and unequivocally. But Jesus was 'full of grace and truth', and his church needs to bear witness to the truth while exhibiting the grace that makes the truth an achievable goal rather than a judgmental ideal.

The second characteristic of Remnant Theology which keeps churches small is a low expectation for growth. This is almost always built on experience and is particularly hard to find in parts of the world that are experiencing or have recently experienced revival. The Baptist preacher and evangelist C. H. Spurgeon was reportedly asked by a younger preacher why he was not as successful as Spurgeon in his evangelism. Spurgeon answered along the lines that surely the young man didn't expect someone to get saved every time he preached, to which the young man modestly replied, 'of course not'. Spurgeon closed the discussion with the observation, 'Well, there's your problem'.

Finally, Remnant Theology removes the responsibility of evangelism from the church or individual, and it does this with an overemphasis on God's sovereignty. The word sovereignty has only appeared in recent translations of the Bible where it is used in preference to 'almighty'. The Greek word for 'almighty' (*pantokrator*) is derived from the word *krator*, which signifies the presence of force and

24

strength, not its exercise. It is static, not dynamic. Any study of the ideas of God's authority soon shows that God has delegated aspects of his authority to his creation for us to exercise in a dynamic way.

God has taken responsibility for mankind's redemption by sending his son to die and by sending his Holy Spirit. It is purely laziness that causes a church to shirk its responsibility and echo the words spoken to William Carey, 'When God chooses to convert the heathen he will do so without our help.'

The elements that go into bad theological reasons for smallness were perfectly summed up by an incident I witnessed while preparing for an open-air event in the centre of a large Midlands town. Two evangelists had beaten us to our pitch. One of them wore a sandwich board with, 'for all I have sinned . . .' on one side and 'repent' on the other. The second evangelist had brought a heavy wooden pulpit which elevated him above contradiction and shielded him from approach. He started to preach on the apostasy of the surrounding society with accompanying dramatic arm movements. A group of teenagers tried to get his attention, but he resolutely ignored them. They tried harder and harder until eventually they were lined up either side of him repeating his words and flailing their arms too. I asked his companion why they were there. Instead of taking the opportunity to evangelize me, he simply told me that God had told them to come and preach and that they would go when God told them to stop.

They had not come to preach because they felt responsible to carry the good news to the people of this town. They had come because they felt it was something that Christians ought to do. They had no expectation of making any meaningful contact with the crowd and their exclusivity was evidenced by the barriers of sandwich board and pulpit that they had put between themselves and those they were attempting to preach to.

This is an easy case to criticize, but the same principles are at work in many small congregations. A few years ago the 'Churches Together' in one town initiated a town-wide mission. The mission team went to visit one Free Church to encourage their participation, only to be told by the leader with considerable satisfaction, 'When I came here twenty years ago, we had fifty people. We still have fifty people.' This church didn't want to be involved because they had no desire to grow, they were comfortable with their size and they couldn't see the point of joining in with other churches in the area. This is a far more common manifestation of these same principles.

Many congregations are small because a subtle form of Remnant Theology has caused them to focus on their own needs. It is not at all uncommon for a leader to look at the congregation and think, 'With all these needs there is no way we can initiate outreach activities.' A few years back, a popular teaching actually supported this way of thinking. It went something like this: 'If we build a body of people who really love each other, unbelievers will be magnetically drawn to the quality of our lives together. Therefore, we will concentrate on meeting the needs of the Christians and developing a higher quality of life. As we succeed, outsiders will flock in.'

But they didn't. In reality, the more a church concentrates on its own pastoral needs, the more overwhelming those needs become.

Jesus likened the Kingdom of God to a mustard seed. Though it may appear small and insignificant, it is destined for growth. Without a vision for growth, both numerically and in maturity, no church can be healthy for long. An outward-looking, growth-expecting, missionary attitude should be a central part of the philosophy of ministry of every local church.

Western culture

Small churches can also be an effect of our Western culture. The Church is a community, yet for more than 400 years, Western culture has been elevating the importance of the individual at the expense of the community. Up until the Age of Reason, a person's value and identity had been found in the community, and his or her knowledge was derived from the community. Descartes' celebrated phrase, '*Cogito, ergo sum*', ('I think therefore I am') summarized in three words the ferment in Western thinking and cultural understanding of the period. In a single sentence he had shifted the source of modern man's identity and knowledge to the individual. Of course the whole of our modern world view does not flow from this statement alone, but it sums up the ferment in Western thinking at the time, a ferment that was to lay the foundation for our modern world.

The newly invented printing press was carrying this revolution into the church, as individuals could now read the Bible in the privacy of their own rooms, though it had in the main been written to be read to groups of people. Promises that were meant for a corporate 'you' could be taken for the individual.

The cult of the individual can be seen in all aspects of life. Our basis for morals has shifted from the benefit of society to an individual's rights, from concern for our neighbours to protection of the self. As the technology which was the fruit of this new way of thinking has developed, it has enabled us to live more and more of our lives in isolation. Now our opinions are more likely to be formed by mass media than local consensus.

Sociologists have noticed that we are forming fewer intimate friendships. This in part explains the popularity of soap operas; we have lost the skills to be close to our neighbours, so we join in the lives of their TV substitutes.

The consequences for Church life are two-fold. First, new Christians may find the level of relationship in a local congregation alien and intimidating. In addition, those already in the congregation may be resistant to growth that would threaten intimacy.

The trend towards isolation shows no sign of abating. I am writing this in my home on a computer, and as I complete a chapter I can send it to my co-author over the phone lines for his amendments. I can also use this computer to do my shopping, banking, make flight reservations, trade on the stock market, review today's papers and a lot more. Soon the combination of computer, phone and television will come together to remove even more of those inconvenient activities that bring us into contact with others living around us. I will no longer have to walk to the video shop to hire a video to watch in the privacy of my own home. Instead, I will be able to dial up a video service, select the desired film on my computer and have it instantly down-loaded to my television.

I am not doing these things because I don't want to be a part of a community, but in doing them I lose the skills necessary to be a fruitful part of one. People still crave good neighbourly relationships. People cannot stop being 'social animals' because at the heart of God is relationship. Before God ever made a decision, he was in relationship, Father, Son and Holy Spirit, and we are in his image. It follows that, if relationship is at the heart of the gospel and our culture is not very good at relationship, then evangelism and integration of new Christians into a church will be harder than in less Westernized parts of the world.

We are also more likely to feel content with very small congregations and unsure with large ones. When one network of cells recently restructured to give itself fewer but larger congregations, a number of long-standing Christians left specifically because they wanted to be part of a congregation of less than fifty members.

Paradoxically, however, small congregations are often more threatening to the new member than large ones. They can appear to demand an immediate depth of relationship with a group that is already at ease with itself. On the other hand, in a slightly larger group the new member can maintain a degree of anonymity without fear of never being able to make friends. Analysis of the 1989 English Church Census has shown that the average size of a growing Protestant church was 123 and that churches with over 100 adult attenders were nearly four times more likely to be growing than those with less than 100. It is very rare to find a large church nowadays that has not adopted a cell system of some type. Unlike the small church, the cells or house groups are often changing and are therefore easier to join than a group whose long-term relationships have made it an unintentional clique. The mass meetings provide a safe place for the new Christian to learn without too much commitment, while the small group provides the means by which they can be integrated into the church community when they are ready.

These cultural dynamics are things that churches must recognize and find ways to address. For the large church, the solutions may seem easy. But for small congregations, keeping themselves open to new Christians without overpowering them is an exercise that requires the co-operation and spiritual growth of most members.

Finally, it is obvious that there are sometimes accidental reasons why churches are small. Just as churches can be small for good strategic reasons, changing demographics can leave a church small quite by accident.

During the 1970s, one London borough used to operate an apartheid-like housing policy, while incidentally renaming its streets to honour those who opposed apartheid in South Africa. As a result, the 1991 UK census showed that the borough had broken into three areas. The south-east, dominated by white-priority housing estates, had almost no ethnic population. The mid-west was predominantly owner-occuped and racially mixed. The north was mainly ethnic-priority housing estates. It is still possible to find a number of small, ageing white congregations in the north of the borough in places where less than a quarter of the population are of Anglo-Saxon origin. The Church as a whole is growing across the whole borough, but these churches have little opportunity to take advantage of this tendency.

The above are bad or accidental reasons for being small. In all of them smallness is a consequence of various forces rather than a means for further growth. None of them, however, necessarily makes a church an unpleasant place to be. While these churches may not actively contribute to completing the Great Commission, most of them won't detract from it either.

THE UGLY

Sadly there are situations where churches are small for reasons that do detract from the Church fulfilling its destiny. If there is an effectiveness in missions that comes with unity, and if there is a hindrance that comes with division and sin. In general we can divide ugly reasons for a lack of church growth into two types, individual sin in leadership and corporate sin in a congregation. Leadership sin is potentially far more damaging than congregational sin, but congregational sin is no less effective at preventing a church from reaching its God-appointed destiny.

Sadly, leadership sin furnishes us with countless lurid examples. We can site situations where after years of decline, it is discovered that a leader has been sexually abusing or having affairs with members of the youth group or congregation. In the light of the subsequent damage to people's lives and faith, it is not surprising that the Lord does not allow these churches to grow.

Unfortunately there is a line of thought that attempts to separate a leader's sin from his or her ability to lead. We could fill this section with stories where the decision to 'cover' a leader's sin has caused far more grief and pain than if it had been exposed earlier. It is not within the scope of this book to deal with how a church copes with sin in its leadership. It is enough to say that while this reason for lack of growth is not normal, it is not uncommon. In a survey of American evangelical leaders carried out by *Leadership* magazine, 12 per cent admitted to extra-marital intercourse while they were ministers and 23 per cent admitted to some other form of inappropriate sexual conduct. And it estimated that these figures are rising. It is naïve to assume that Europe is immune to similar problems.

Most typical of ugly reasons why churches are small are the sins related to pride and division. These are well illustrated by a church that we will call 'Harlington Free Church'. The members of Harlington Free Church knew each other well. Many of them had been members together for twenty years or more. When I met them, they numbered about thirty adults with half that number of children. I was there as a guest preacher for the weekend and I found myself addressing a positive and attentive congregation. However, as I engaged in private conversation with several members, it became obvious that appearances were deceptive. This was not a positive group of people. It was increasingly hard for most of them to keep their spirits up because they could remember a time when the congregation had been twice as large.

The church had been led by four elders, but a job change and a retirement had halved the leadership team. The two remaining elders seemed like a great pair. One (we shall call him Ron) owned and managed a small but successful business and his organizational and leadership abilities were obvious. The other elder (James) had developed a fine Bible-teaching ministry and was much in demand at other churches, although he was careful to control his speaking schedule so that it reflected his primary commitment to Harlington Free Church. In addition, there were a good number of responsible, mature Christians in the congregation and there was plenty of scope for expanding the leadership team. Everything looked good and healthy and yet the church was declining.

Over lunch with James and his wife, I learned that, on a number of issues, they didn't see eye to eye with Ron. They were gracious and guarded in the way they spoke, but it appeared there was little common ground between James and Ron. That evening I had an open and honest talk with Ron, who confirmed that he was not happy with James's position on several subjects. He felt that James was trying to introduce too many changes to the church.

I offered to come back a few weeks later to see if we could find a way ahead. It seemed that God had granted me favour with these two men, in that both of them had been very honest and trusting as we spoke. I was sure we could find ground for reconciliation and progress.

On my next visit I asked questions and listened to other members of the church. I was rather discouraged to find that most of the members had already aligned themselves with either Ron or James. In the evening I got together with Ron and James to talk about the issues. What an exhausting evening! They disagreed about everything. James wanted to add to the eldership, Ron thought no one was ready yet. James wanted to introduce changes and new freedom into the meetings. Ron wanted them to stay as they were. James wanted to join in an interchurch outreach in the town, Ron did not think they could identify with some of the other churches to that extent.

At one point, Ron lost his temper and shouted at James. Then he turned to me, and as I looked into his red face, veins bulging, I began to doubt that there was a way ahead. After he had calmed down, we decided that I should meet further with Ron the next day.

We talked through several issues again, this time without anger. But there was no progress. Ron had very clear and strong opinions about the church and what it should be doing and he was not prepared to compromise on any issues. When I reported back to James, we agreed that if the church was going to continue, Ron would have to lead it and James would have to decide whether or not he could support him. After much heart-searching over a period of weeks, James decided he could support Ron and would trust God to take the church forward under Ron's leadership.

After further prayer, I went back to Ron to say, 'If you are convinced this is the way forward for the church, then you will have to take responsibility for it and give more time to leading it.' I explained how James was unable to lead the church in the direction Ron wanted, but was prepared to give full support to Ron's leadership. Ron did not feel God was calling him to take further leadership, nor was he prepared to support James in leadership. But there seemed to be no one else in the congregation who would be capable of leading the church in the direction wanted.

Finally, after several months of work, I had to go to Ron and say, 'I don't see a way for Harlington Free Church to survive. The rift between you and James cannot be bridged at this time.' Once again I felt the force of Ron's temper. After he had calmed down, he reluctantly concluded that there was no alternative – the church would have to close.

Harlington Free Church was small for an ugly reason. In the end it died. Jesus said 'By this will all men know that you are my disciples, if you love one another' (John 13:35). This is especially vital in the lives of the leaders of the church. Differences of opinion will arise; misunderstandings and friction may occur. But true unity emerges when the people involved maintain a commitment to work things out.

If Harlington Free Church had been small simply because differences of opinion had left it directionless, then it would have been small for a bad reason. But these differences had brought into the open an ugly stubbornness that would rather see the church die than change. If suspicion, distrust, anger and hurt become rooted in the leadership of a church, that church cannot fulfil its calling. If those attitudes cannot be resolved, then that church has no right to exist. These may sound like harsh words, but misrepresenting Jesus is a very serious matter.

In the case of Harlington Free Church the sin of pride was easy to identify, yet this same sin holds many churches back from growth. In 2 Tim 3, Paul warns about difficult times brought about by sinful men whose list of sins include being 'lovers of self . . . arrogant . . . ungrateful . . . irreconcilable . . . conceited'. This love of the self is fostered by European culture with its worship of the individual. We end up with church leaders who will not be led, struggling with churches full of people who will only follow when they agree with their decisions.

When the Israelites continually complained about Moses' leadership, God accused them of sinning against himself. In the end, neither Moses nor those Israelites actually made it into the promised land.

Some congregations have had their growth stifled by this type of vision-robbing arrogance at all levels of church life. The Church's job is to fill up the earth and Jesus tells us it is the meek who are going to achieve this goal. Leaders need to model this meekness by mutual submission within their leadership teams, as well as to leaders from other congregations and by an openness to the ideas and misgivings of the congregation. Church members need to learn how to follow their leadership in all decisions that do not directly contravene scripture. Many congregations have been diverted from evangelism to deal with factions demanding a change in the time of the service, or objecting to changes in the décor. It is the conviction of the authors that, nine times out of ten, the Church would experience more growth if they would get on with pursuing a common vision, rather than debating its finer details.

In reviewing ugly reasons why congregations are small, we have focused on sin. It is important to remember that the more extreme examples make obvious illustrations. But Paul lists gossiping, ingratitude and lack of forgiveness alongside adultery, brutality and love of money in his list of the characteristics of those who will bring difficult times on the Church (2 Tim 3:1-6). Integrity in leadership and commitment to each other are crucial for a congregation to achieve its potential.

3

HOW SMALL IS SMALL?

In Chapter 1 we gave a qualitative definition of the small church: it is a gathering of people in a network of relationships to express a common life in Jesus in a locale. In Chapter 4, we will begin to explore the purpose of the Church in human history and destiny. Before we do that we must examine the nature of the Church a little further and try to understand what makes a gathering a local church. We also want to discover how small a local church can be and still be involved in the Great Commission?

Liberal thinkers and liberal theologians have long held that Jesus did not intend to start a church. The reasoning behind this is that Jesus preaches almost entirely about 'the Kingdom'. He refers to his church on only two occasions in the Gospels. In *Jesus and the Gospel Tradition* C. K. Barret argues that Jesus' teaching on the Kingdom amounted to an imminent eschatology that allowed no time for the emergence of an organized structure. Quoting an earlier commentator, he sums up his view with the assertion, 'Jesus foretold the Kingdom and it was the Church that came.' Certainly, even the most basic ecclesiastic structures have more to do with Paul than they do with Jesus; and even Paul's structures appear to be inconsistent, sometimes referring to deacons, elders and overseers and other times writing about evangelists, pastors and apostles.

A full exploration of the relationship between the

Church and the Kingdom is not possible at this point, but some comment is necessary.

WHERE DID THE CHURCH COME FROM?

The Greek word *ekklesia*, normally translated 'church' in our bibles, originally had no such theologically loaded meaning. In Tyndale's first English translation of the Bible the word *ekklesia* was translated throughout as 'congregation' with the exception of Acts 19:37, where it refers to 'heathen churches'. In this same passage, *ekklesia* is used to describe the rioting mob at Ephesus and then the city's legal assembly. When translated literally, *ekklesia* is simply a group that is 'called out' or 'called forth', although it was often used to refer to religious communities of different deities. So, in the New Testament, we find the frequent qualifications 'of God' or 'of Christ'. More importantly, *ekklesia* was the Greek word to describe the 'assembly' or 'congregation' of Israel in the Septuagint version of the Old Testament, before they had achieved nationhood (Deut 4:10, 9:10, 18:16, 31:30). With this in mind, it is obvious that, to an early Christian, the word 'church' would not simply imply a static congregation, let alone a building. It would have carried ideas of a group progressing from somewhere to a promised destiny.

Another important concept to the New Testament understanding of church was fellowship or community (*Koinonia*). Jesus' teaching on aspects of relationship are foundational to this idea. Howard Snyder comments in *The Community of King* that 'if peoplehood underlies the continuity of the God's plan from the Old to New Testament, community calls attention to the "new covenant", the "new wine" '.

If we accept that the Church of Jesus Christ is simply the fellowship of those who are 'called forth' by him, then it is easy to see that teaching about the nature and structure of the church is implicit in Jesus' words and lifestyle. The last words of Jesus in Matthew were, 'Teach them to observe all that I commanded you,' so they went out and started churches everywhere. Fundamental to all that Jesus had taught them was the need to be 'in church'. Church was the place of discipleship, and therefore making disciples meant first starting churches.

We often refer to Pentecost as the birthday of the Church. However, it may be more helpful to see Pentecost as a barmitzvah, a public presentation of something that was born when Jesus first called disciples to himself.

WHAT MAKES A CHURCH A CHURCH?

If the Church was instigated by Jesus and his teaching relates to it, then it is a relatively easy matter to answer the question, 'What makes a gathering a church, or at what point does the church start?' The answer can be found in Jesus' two explicit references to his *ekklesia*.

And if your brother sins, go and reprove him in private; if he listens to you, you have won your brother. But if he does not listen to you, take one or two more with you, so that by the mouth of two or three witnesses every fact may be confirmed. And if he refuses to listen to them, tell it to the church; and if he refuses to listen even to the church, let him be to you as a Gentile or tax-gatherer. Truly I say to you, whatever you shall bind in earth shall be bound in heaven; and whatever you shall loose on earth shall be loosed in heaven. Again I say to you, that if two of you agree on earth about anything that they may ask, it shall be done for them by my Father who is in heaven. For where two or three are gathered in my name I am in the midst.' (Matt 18:15-20)

In Matt 18:17, Jesus teaches that disputes between his disciples should be brought before the church for resolution. All of Matt 18 is a collection of teaching on order and discipline within the community of disciples. These particular verses teach us that there is an authority in the coming together of disciples (Matt 18:16, 17). If there is disunity between two, then it should be sorted out, because their authority and power rests on their agreement (Matt 18:19, 20). If the issue can't be easily resolved it must be tested against the wider unity of the church, first 'two or three witnesses' and then the whole body. The power and authority, lost by the disagreeing couple, restored by the 'two or three witnesses' and represented by the Church, is the presence of Jesus himself (Matt 18:20).

This passage shows us that the presence and authority of Jesus are as real in a group of two or three as in a group of 100, and that Jesus' Church starts with two or three coming together in his name to exercise his authority.

It is interesting to note that, when Jesus sends out his seventy disciples to 'every city and place where he himself was going to come' (Luke 10:1), he sends them out in pairs and tells them to find a third person from the locale before they can do any preaching, healing, etc. Jesus' disciples were effectively establishing embryonic churches to contain the authority and presence of the imminent Messiah.

The reason for labouring this point is that it has been argued that a church is a church because of its leadership structure: Bishop, priest and deacon in the main historic denominations; pastor and elder in other denominations; and apostle, prophet, evangelist, pastor and teacher in the more radical traditions. This happens because the Church has been traced back to its apostolic foundation, but not to its Messianic initiation. Even so, if we consider that throughout the New Testament phrases like 'the brethren', 'the disciples' and 'those being saved' are used interchangeably with 'church', it becomes clear that, even in a purely post-Pentecost definition of the Church, the community of disciples is more foundational than any structure.

This is a very important conclusion. If a small church is to play its part in missions, it will need to be free from any obligation to support an ecclesiastic structure that might be more suited to life in a larger congregation.

The idea that the hallmarks of Jesus' Church are his revealed presence and the exercise of his authority are also found in Jesus' only other explicitly recorded reference to his Church.

> He said to them, 'who do you say that I am?' And Simon Peter answered and said, 'You are the Christ, the son of the living God.' And Jesus answered and said to him, 'Blessed are you Simon Barjona, because flesh and blood did not reveal this to you, but my Father who is in heaven. And I also say to you that you are Peter, and upon this rock I will build my church and the gates of Hades shall not overpower it. I will give you the keys of the Kingdom of heaven, and whatever you shall loose on earth shall be loosed in heaven' (Matt 16:15-19).

It has been explained on many occasions, even by Roman Catholic theologians, that despite the deliberate word play on Simon's nickname, 'the rock', these verses contain the revelation of Jesus as 'the Son of God' and all the truths that flow from that fact. While this cannot be incontrovertibly proved from these verses, this is clearly the way Peter understood the words 'this rock' and passed it on to us. In his first letter, Peter portrays Jesus as the foundation and corner stone of God's new temple, with Peter and all other disciples as other stones within the building. (1 Pet 2:4-8).

In both passages above, it is an identification with the person of Jesus that characterizes his Church. We are not 'Godians' or 'Biblians', the Church is a 'Christian' assembly. The passage in Matt 16 also shows that the exercise of authority is a characteristic of the Church. That authority extends beyond human relationships, all the way to the gates of hell. Furthermore, this exercise of authority relates to the extension of the Kingdom of Heaven, with which so much of Jesus' teaching is preoccupied.

From these two dominical references to the Church of Jesus Christ, a picture of the Church starts to emerge. It is a picture which, if space allowed, could be shown to be both consistent and supported by the rest of scripture. At its heart is community, although the Church is more than just a community. It is a community on the move, defined by the revelation of who Jesus is and his presence in the lives of its members. Its purpose is to continue revealing Jesus and to exercise his authority as administrators of God's Kingdom. Revealing Jesus and exercising his authority are the building blocks of the Church's mission.

It therefore follows that a congregation that is not involved in missions is not a proper local church, whatever its size and whatever its structure. Reverend Dr Stuart Murray, who lectures at Spurgeons College in London, has gone so far as to say that the term 'para-church' would be more appropriately applied to congregations that have no mission focus rather than to mission agencies getting on with the Church's primary function of mission. The Church is a congregation of people on the basis of who Jesus is in order to manifest his presence and exercise his authority, and it starts with two or three coming together.

SO WHY BOTHER WITH CHURCH STRUCTURES?

Of course churches have always had structures: a comparison of the three lists of the twelve disciples would indicate that even they were grouped into three teams of four, with Peter, Philip and James as team leaders. Leadership is crucial to a successful local congregation. But if structures are not what makes a group of people a local church, then what are they for?

Howard Snyder explains the relationship between a church's structure, its mission and its underlying community nicely in *The Community of the King*. He writes, 'Biblically, the Church is the community of God's people and this is a spiritual reality which is valid in every culture. But all ecclesiastical institutions – whether seminaries, denominational structures, mission boards, publishing houses or what have you – are not the Church. Rather, they are supportive institutions created to serve the Church in its life and mission.' This is an extremely important conclusion: in the authors' opinions, the only really justifiable one.

The word 'church' is used in the New testament to refer to all the believers in a town, city or region as well as to a group in someone's home. Paul writes about all sorts of church structures and procedures. The range of uses of the word 'church' in the New Testament should not be a problem to us. In *Cinderella with Amnesia*, Michael Griffiths parallels the word 'church' with the word 'moon', which we use 'whether we are viewing the full moon, the half moon or even the slenderest of crescent moons. In fact . . . it is impossible to see it all at once. In the same way, we never see the whole Church; yet even when we see only a small part of it, it is still correct to say, "look there is the Church." '

The Church is the community of discipleship. Since its inception, the Church has developed various support structures which broadly fall into two categories: those that primarily aid the local expression of the Church, and those that primarily enable its wider expression. The former include elders, churchwardens, treasurers, pastors and parish Christian councils; the latter include denominations, bishops, missions and evangelistic agencies. Some structures, such as Christian publishers and national conferences, may be of equal benefit to both. Of course, certain structures will seem more important than others and some are more effective than others.

A lot of this may seem like arguing over semantics. However, there are wide-ranging issues at stake in our understanding of the responsibilities and authority of a particular group of believers. When Christians come together in an office prayer meeting or school Christian Union, they carry full responsibility for bringing the Kingdom of God to that place and making disciples in that place. Their responsibility and authority are no different than that of the parish church for its parish.

On a campus of 5000 people, it is not wrong to consider the Christian Union the primary expression of the Church to that college or university. It has been said that a CU can't be a church because it has a narrow age range and high turnover of members. However, there are hundreds of local churches that would also not qualify if the same criteria were applied to them.

It has also been argued that the existence of a particular kind of structure, namely that of missions agencies, is a God-ordained institution with a parallel or extra responsibility to the Church for the accomplishment of the Great Commission. A big deal is often made of the fact that in Acts 13 the Holy Spirit 'sends out' Paul and Barnabas whereas the church simply 'let them go'. It is claimed that these verses constitute a divine ordination of a new structure. This is weak logic. A specific instruction by the Holy Spirit can hardly be taken as a mandate for a second institution with the primary mandate for mission. Of course, half the problem is that the Church has been seen as a local structure.

If we have not accepted that the Church is made up only of people in local structures, then it is easy to see how the Holy Spirit led the early disciples to start operating more widely. The pattern is not new: it is Jesus' two or three together in his name (in this case Paul, Barnabas and John), being sent out to the places that Jesus is going to come to. Furthermore, this missionary team is not independent of the local church. They constitute some of its main leadership, and this leadership is exercised on their return in Acts 15, where they call the church together to report on their success. Similarly, when their missionary work brings the issue of Gentile observance of the law into contention, the entire church leadership is brought together in Jerusalem to decide on the issue. When Paul sets out with Silas for his second missionary trip he is again committed to God's grace by the Antioch church.

Dividing the Church into two independent institutions is unhelpful. It leads to situations where local churches adopt missionaries rather than send them, or simply take a collection and send a contribution to an expert body who carry the real responsibility for the Great Commission. If we accept Howard Snyder's conclusions, then the responsibility for the Great Commission remains with every house group, Christian Union, congregation and missionary organization. A missionary society should simply be a structure that resources and enables the whole Church in its God-given, world-wide evangelistic responsibility.

The relationship between the local church and mission agencies is something that the Holy Spirit seems to be speaking about in all sorts of places. As we approach the end of this millennium, a world-wide network of mission agencies and churches has been formed. It is called the 'AD 2000 and Beyond' movement. The motto of AD 2000 is 'The whole Church taking the whole Gospel to the whole world'. In order to achieve their objectives, these networked agencies are seeking to mobilize local churches in their responsibility for missions. In addition, on the denominational side the Council of Churches for Britain and Ireland is looking at how to restructure the local congregations of the historic denominations in order to be ready for missions in the new millennium.

Whatever the outcome of all these plans and processes, the unity of purpose and active co-operation between local church structures and wider structures – which include denominations, ecumenical church networks and mission societies, is a fulfilment, in part, of Jesus' prayer that we should be one, so that the world might believe.

CELL, CONGREGATION OR CELEBRATION?

The answer to the question posed at the beginning of this chapter, 'how small can a local church be and still be involved in the Great Commission?' is that a church can be any size as long as it is willing to work in partnership. If it is not willing, then it will have to develop structures that are inappropriate to the local fellowship, which in all likelihood will be the death of it. The success of the new denominations in the UK and in the United States in recent years is partly due to the close co-operation between the local churches and the wider leadership, often called the 'Apostolic Team'. This close co-operation, rather than loose affiliation, is one of the distinguishing factors between a movement and an institution.

A good, easily understood example of how co-operation with the wider church in an area enables the small church to take part more effectively in missions might be the city-wide crusades of evangelists like Billy Graham. A significant section of the church in the city will come together as the organizers of the crusade, and between them provide the finances, the administration, and the councillors required. Where this process often falls short is that this manifestation of the city-wide church is a temporary hiccup until such time as 'normal services' can be resumed.

On the other hand, local ecumenical groups often provide an ongoing expression of unity. Sadly, however, it is very rarely a unity built on mission, which is the purpose for which Jesus prayed for his disciples' unity (John 18:20-26). What is needed is the blending of these two models. Local churches need to find ways of expressing their co-operation in continuing evangelistic activity. This need not always be in common events or a joint programme.

As part of the DAWN strategy in England, the co-ordinators have been encouraging churches all over the country to join together in local versions of the national DAWN strategy. Such local strategies could be called 'Disciple A Whole Neighbourhood' instead of 'Disciple A Whole Nation'. In these local or district DAWN strategies, churches work together to develop a long-term plan of prayer, research, leadership training, church planting and evangelism to make sure that everyone in the local area is continually hearing the gospel. The co-operation involved in these strategies is opening up all sorts of evangelistic possibilities to all sorts and sizes of church.

In one of the first such strategies, the joint research undertaken by local churches in a town highlighted their failure to reach the town's young people. In fact, only a Pentecostal church was having any success at all in this area, and they were soon to lose their youth pastor because of lack of finance. When this came to light, a local Roman Catholic priest volunteered to find the finances required. For a whole year the town had a Pentecostal evangelist who was financed by the local Roman Catholic church.

In a second situation, a congregation of fifty is thrilled that their premises, which can take 900, are being used for area prayer celebrations focused on the evangelization of the town. In a third town, a couple of smaller churches are being 'lent' some trainee evangelists for a year by a larger church. In a fourth, a church of around fifty is co-ordinating a city-wide outreach for over 100 trainee evangelists from an international agency. The evangelists will work with and be accommodated by a number of other churches in the city-wide DAWN network.

Today, most of the world's largest and fastest growing local churches are what are often called cell churches. These are churches made up of thousands of local cells that relate together across the wider area with each cell having between five and twenty members. The key to understanding their success, say the commentators, is that each cell is considered to be a fully functioning local church operating in a well-defined area. The cell carries the same responsibility for evangelism, teaching and so on as the wider network, but to a smaller and more precise degree. What the cell churches have shown is that a small congregation need not be limited in its growth if it can free itself from unhelpful structures and find ways of linking in with the resources and spiritual impetus that belong to the larger expressions of church life.

There is a children's chorus that ends with the lines, 'in this world of darkness, we must let it shine, you in your small corner and I in mine'. World mission is made up of millions of 'small corner' missions, but just as coals stop glowing if they lose contact with other coals, our evangelistic endeavours can lose their impact if they are viewed and undertaken with a 'small corner mentality', rather than a God's-eye view of the wider picture. Environmentalists have a saying 'Think global, act local'; a church of any size can get involved with world mission, whether a cell, a congregation or a celebration, but first they need to see the master plan and the other players so that they can understand and make the most of their contribution.

4

THE ROLE OF THE SMALL CHURCH IN EVENGELISM

Since its inception in 1975, the DAWN strategy has been drawing attention to the importance of the local church in world mission. No previous missions strategy had so clearly identified the crucial role of the small, local, contextually relevant church as DAWN. The principles which shape a 'Disciple A Whole Nation' strategy have been fully described by its initiator Jim Montgomery in *DAWN 2000: 7,000,000 Churches To Go*. In this chapter, we let Wolfgang Fernandez who facilitates DAWN in Europe explain the importance of the local church in the evangelization of an area. He has had extensive personal experience of church planting in California and in his own ministry as a missionary on three continents. His experiences have been analysed and illustrate issues to be taken into account.

BY THE LIGHT OF DAWN

Danilo Colmenares and his wife and children arrived in San Jose, California to find themselves completely alone in a totally different culture. Danilo was in a place where he could barely understand the language which would enable him to buy food and take care of the basic necessities for himself and his family.

SMALL CHURCH, BIG VISION

As he was feeling alone and totally lost, my family along with other people from our church, met him. We decided to try to reach new families in the apartment complex he had moved into. We found his family living with no furniture and very few resources of any kind. We immediately took an interest in them and began to demonstrate to this family the love of the Lord Jesus Christ. We provided some furniture for his living room, a table and chairs for their meals and beds for the children. We were also able to bring food so that their immediate needs could be taken care of. This family was very thankful and appreciative of these strangers who had come claiming to be doing all these good deeds in the name of a God – a God whom they knew only in a very distant fashion.

As we got to know them better, they began to understand more about the God whom we loved and served. As they observed the reality of our faith, they were attracted and adopted our faith more and more as time went on. Danilo was not the sort of person who would normally be open to hear the gospel of Jesus Christ. But his circumstances helped to create a receptivity. As a major in the Nicaraguan army, he had trained himself to be a self-sufficient person and exercised much power and influence in his country. After the Sandinistas took over the government of his country, Danilo had to flee for his life. And so, he came to find himself and his family completely alone in the United States. As our small congregation met his most pressing needs, we were able to practise the love of Christ in the best way we could and give Danilo a sense of family and belonging, something that he and his family were desperately lacking.

As we observe the landscape of the Church around the world, we find that the majority of the churches are churches like our little church in San Jose. Various research

50

studies have shown that the single-cell church is the most common expression of the Body of Christ around the world. According to the Operation World statistics, gathered by Patrick Johnston, the average church in the world is made up of 147 persons. In the United States, for several years that average has been seventy-five regular church attendants, while in one of the areas of fastest growth in the world – Latin America – the average number is eighty-eight. As a general rule, Latin America and some parts of Asia share the same average. In Africa and India, the number of regular attendants is closer 150, while most Western nations, including Australia and New Zealand, have a lower average. In Europe, a recent study done by DAWN Europa in Germany indicates that the average size of the church in that country is forty-four people.

One of the most significant strengths of the single-cell church is to be found in evangelism. Since it generally tends to have a narrow focus of ministry, it is able to meet the need to feel part of a 'family'. Single-cell churches are usually made up of people who tend to identify with each other in a strong homogeneous setting and can thus offer very personal support. It is widely known that loneliness is a major felt need in urban settings, where people often live independently from one another and are disconnected from their roots and their home towns. A small, local congregation has the potential to bring urban dwellers to faith in the Lord Jesus Christ and to provide the family identity that they long to have. In the absence of other family, the church becomes the place where they come to celebrate triumphs, cope with crisis, or endure hardship as a result of their new faith in Jesus Christ. This is what attracted our friend Danilo to our local congregation.

In rural centres, where traditions are stronger and where family unit tends to be more cohesive, the local church can provide a safe haven for those who have made a decision for Jesus Christ which may not be accepted or approved of by their relatives, friends or neighbours. In other words, in rural settings the church provides a new identity for people who have come to know the Lord Jesus Christ, thus fulfilling the same sociological need for a 'family' identification.

THE REALITY OF THE SMALL CHURCH IN EFFECTIVE EVANGELISM

It is important to clarify what we mean by effective evangelism. We are concerned with the growth of churches, especially single-cell churches. So we are obviously interested in more than just 'decisions for Christ'. We are concerned with those who have made a commitment to Jesus and have been incorporated into the life of a local congregation. To understand effective evangelism, I believe we need to have regard for the Great Commission and review the specific instructions that the Lord Jesus Christ gave his disciples. Matt 28:19, 20 states that the Lord commissioned His followers to 'make disciples of all nations'.

Jesus then goes on to explain how disciples were to be made. First of all, he says, 'baptizing them in the name of the Father, the Son and the Holy Spirit'. The act of baptism, as generally practised in churches today, implies a recognition by those baptized that a clear commitment has been made to follow the Lord Jesus Christ. They have recognized their position as sinners in need of forgiveness, and have understood that this forgiveness can only be found in the substitutionary death of the Lord Jesus Christ on their behalf. Jesus continues to explain this 'disciple-making process' by adding to this task the job of teaching.

He says, 'teaching them to observe all that I commanded you'. The fruit of effective evangelism is evidenced by a decision to demonstrate that commitment through public baptism. That act must be followed by a life-long process of learning to follow Jesus more closely.

Clearly, effective evangelism is a long-term process that happens best within the fellowship of a local congregation. One of the most interesting dynamics that is taking place in missions in the 1990s is the recognition that open-air evangelism taking place in squares, parks or streets of cities and villages around the world is not enough. Large organizations like YWAM, Campus Crusade and the Navigators, in many nations in all continents, have decided to focus their activities towards establishing cells and congregations of believers as the desired outcome of their evangelistic outreaches.

My personal experience with my congregation in San Jose enabled me to see a caring group of people providing an atmosphere of love, support and encouragement to those who were in desperate need. I concluded that the single cell best provides a setting in which people could feel understood and where they could be recognized and encouraged by others.

My first major exposure to the planting of single-cell churches happened in Guatemala where I became involved in encouraging the national leaders and pastors to work towards the development of a national strategy. We wanted a strategy that would aim to cover the whole nation with Bible-believing congregations that were committed to demonstrate the love, care and concern that Jesus has for every individual. The vision was to establish a congregation for every 1000 people in the nation.

As we challenged the Church towards this goal, we sought to understand what the Holy Spirit was already doing in the country. We learned that the Church in Guatemala was experiencing tremendous growth, which was due to quite specific factors. Our research discovered two keys which were providing powerful, sustained, fruitful growth through our efforts of local congregations. The first one was the place that was being given to the scriptures. In Heb 4:14, the Word of God is described as alive and powerful. In Guatemala, we found that growing congregations had a strong and solid commitment to the word of God as the authoritative source of guidance and direction and the place where people could find the ultimate answers for life's major questions. Many of these congregations were amongst people who did not speak Spanish as their mother tongue. In these cases it was vital that the scriptures were available in their own native language.

As we studied the Church in Guatemala, we discovered a second key factor. That proved to be the work of the Holy Spirit. He is the one who gives us the power to be witnesses to Jesus Christ (Acts 1:8). In the Church in Guatemala there was a great emphasis on the presence, power and activity of the Holy Spirit in evangelism. The Guatemalan Christians believed that they would see people touched by God in such a way that their hearts would be opened to the message of the gospel.

It is worth noting that there are large numbers of churches around the world that fervently believe in the Word of God and teach it with great expository clarity. But they are not growing. There are also churches who once experienced a great revival and presence of the Holy Spirit, but as time went on, they have found themselves stuck on a plateau of non-growth. The research that was done in Guatemala and the experience that we have had in nations around the world have shown us a direct correlation between the theological orthodoxy of a congregation and its growth.

One of the most notable examples that we found in Guatemala was the Prince of Peace Church. The founder of this denomination was committed to starting new congregations. He personally started fifty congregations and would constantly remind his followers that the mission of the Church is to plant new churches. He encouraged pastors by insisting that those churches that were not in the process of establishing new ones were experiencing problems. The result of this passion was that in 1980, one in every ten churches in all of Guatemala was part of the Prince of Peace denomination. By that time, there were 610 churches with nearly 40,000 members throughout all but one of the areas of Guatemala. The movement was twenty-seven years old.

Another denomination that was having this kind of experience was the Assemblies of God. Their membership grew a moderate 145 per cent in the ten years from 1970-1980. During that same period the number of Assemblies of God congregations grew 136 per cent. In 1981, the number of congregations grew by 34 per cent in just one year and the total membership increased by a staggering 25 per cent (annual growth rate).

This experience of incredible growth is not limited to Latin America. As we look around the world, this kind of growth is occurring on every continent. An interesting example was reported in the *DAWN Report* magazine of September 1992 by Ted Olson, a team member in DAWN Ministries. He told the story of two churches in Zimbabwe. The City Centre Church was a wonderful worshipping church. People came from everywhere for fellowship in this church, with 1000 people gathered regularly on Sunday mornings. When the City Centre Church lost the lease on its building, the pastors faced a great dilemma, for there were no other places in the main area of the city where they

55

could meet. They had the choice of moving to a distant suburb or starting five or six new churches in the townships around the city. Instead of seeing the group divided into various smaller congregations, they decided to maintain everyone under one roof and one teaching. As a result of this decision, various problems, including transportation difficulties arose, and the City Centre Church has dwindled to only sixty members today.

In contrast, Pastor Solomon of the Alliance Church understood that church multiplication was the only route to survival, so he trained good pastors and lay leaders. In 1989, with a vision and commitment growing strong in his heart, he set goals to see their churches multiplied.

Today, this church has grown from three small congregations of only 100 members, to forty-three churches with 4000 attendance. Sixteen of these churches are in neighbouring Mozambique and Botswana. It is important to note that because of the investment made in training for leadership, all of these churches have their own full-time pastors. This is one of the countless locations where small churches have survived and multiplied while large churches proved to be vulnerable.

In India, where there are 600,000 villages without an evangelical witness, various groups and denominations have committed themselves to seeing 1,000,000 churches planted by the year 2000. One of the groups involved in this vision is a group called Final Thrust 5000. They are working to identify 5000 national missionaries who will be sent into the 400 districts in the nation. The first 1500 have already been sent and are producing an amazing result of 500 new churches a month, or about seventeen per day. The largest of these churches have around 200 members. But the greatest key to their effectiveness is that these churches are being planted by ordinary people everywhere in the country.

The largest denomination in the United States, the Southern Baptists, are aiming to see 50,000 new churches by the year 2000. The last three years they have been planting three churches a day, but now they want to push that further to establish four churches a day for a total of 1500 new churches per year until the year 2000. Dr Larry Lewis, president of the Southern Baptist Home Mission Board, explains that they start new churches not to reach some goals or for some campaign, but to evangelize the nation and to minister to its needs. 'Our real goal,' he said, 'is to see that no human being could be born in these United States and territories who has not had the opportunity to lay hold of the promises of salvation through Jesus Christ, who has not had clear opportunity to become part of a vital Bible-witnessing ministering congregation of people.' As a result of this wonderful commitment, they have targeted 22,000 locations.

The Southern Baptists have discovered that, as they multiply themselves into smaller cells or congregations, their evangelism becomes more effective. An example cited by Dr Lewis is the First Baptist Church of Arlington, which has over 100 missions (new churches) planted in high-rise apartments, government housing projects, ethnic communities and suburban communities. The people of First Baptist Church decided that if they could not get the people to come to church, they would take the church to them. Many of these missions will never have their own building or their own full-time pastor, but they will be a body of baptized believers just as real as the group that meets in an official church building.

This does not mean that small, single-cell churches will inevitably grow. In Europe, as well as on the other continents, we find many stagnant single-cell churches. But there is potential for growth when there is a commitment to start new congregations. The Apostolic Church in Denmark is a good example. From 1980 to 1990 their total attendance growth rate was an unimpressive 4 per cent. At the end of the 1980s, as they developed and began to implement a new vision for church planting, their statistics changed dramatically. At the end of 1990 they commissioned fifteen small groups, primarily made up of young people, to go out and establish new cell groups throughout the country. The result of this evangelistic church planting effort was that by the end of 1991, they saw their attendance growth rate more than double to 10 per cent.

After all these examples, we must deal with the obvious question: Why is it that small churches tend to have a greater evangelistic impact than larger churches? Another example will help us identify the reasons.

The first DAWN-type research study of the church in any community in the United States was made in 1986. It focused on the Santa Clara County and revealed some disturbing realities in this influential part of the world, Silicone Valley. The study of all the Protestant churches in a community of 1,452,230 people revealed that only 4.7 per cent of the population attended church on an average Sunday – just under 97,000 people. This was in spite of appearances, which suggested that the city was full of churches. (This visual misimpression is a common phenomenon.) In fact, the total capacity of the churches in the area was only 160,000, or about 11 per cent of the population. Our research also showed that the churches were running at an average of about half capacity.

Another revealing aspect of this study was the relationship between the different sizes of churches in the community. The large 'mega-churches' in the area were always at the forefront of all the events and their names were known in the media. Their size and impact carried a lot of weight in the community. The average church in the community gave a different perspective: 61 per cent of all the churches in the county had less than 200 people in their congregation. The obvious reality was that the majority of the church-attending population was in these small churches.

Detailed interviews with the pastors of sixty-seven churches, which included all non-denominational churches and a random selection of denominational churches, gave us a good cross-section from the variety of traditions, sizes and geographical locations. Out of these interviews, we were able to note a pattern that showed that many churches right across the spectrum were declining in size. But the smaller churches were having a significant evangelistic impact. We found thirteen churches that had recently been planted and they accounted for 4252 new people attending church. With the exception of two churches, all of these were under 200 in attendance, and a significant percentage of their people were new converts.

This study demonstrated that the new single-cell churches tended to have greater evangelistic potential than any other church. We concluded that the few members of these new churches work harder in evangelism, or else their efforts would come to nothing. It is important to note that we also discovered that converts in the smaller churches tended to migrate to larger churches after a period of time. They seemed to be seeking the encouragement and wide programme that a large church with a multifaceted approach could offer.

The results of our findings are not unique to this area in the United States. In 1979, a study done by Charles Chaney reported in his book *Church Planting at the End of the 20th Century*, showed that Southern Baptist churches between 2000 and 3000 in membership averaged fifty-seven baptisms a year. That same year, the churches with memberships of 200–300 averaged seven baptisms. Ten of the smaller churches (200–300 members) would have baptized thirteen more people than one large church (200–300). In Illinois, small churches with attendances up to 100 baptize four people each year. Larger churches with 1500–1999 in membership average fifty-three baptisms. Thirty churches with fifty members each would have won to Christ almost 300 per cent more people than one church with 1500 members.

Some of the most spectacular church growth anywhere in the world is taking place in India. A recent study compiled the results of 1040 students who had been trained to plant small churches. Between 1985 and 1992, they were able to start more than 87,000 small congregations. These churches averaged between thirty and sixty regular attenders, with 95 per cent of converts coming from a completely different religious background such as Hinduism or Islam.

This huge evangelistic impact by small churches has some common characteristics:

1. New single–cell churches can evangelize better than established churches. One of the primary reasons for this is survival. These small churches must be very active in their evangelism or they will dry up and die. The motivation level for those who start new churches is high and is focused on reaching the lost. Though small churches lack breadth of programme and variety of ministries, they usually have a loving and caring atmosphere and are able to provide a safe haven for new converts or those with an interest in the gospel.

2. The family atmosphere provides an effective environment for assimilation of new people. The small church is able to care for people as individuals. Such personalized attention means that new people have a deeper sense of

belonging than they would have in a very large group of people. Eventually, a single-cell church has a tendency to plateau at an optimum size (perhaps between fifty and one hundred people, depending on a variety of factors). Once this size is reached, the most effective next step for growth is to divide the cell, thus creating another small congregation.

3. This environment provides a place where new leaders can gain experience and credibility fairly quickly. People who have not been able to receive training at a Bible school or seminary, can receive personalized biblical instruction and first-hand experience in their home church. Many people who are trained in this manner can successfully start new small congregations without having more extensive experience.

4. Single-cell churches are in a unique position to overcome the challenge of finding a place to meet. Our study of Santa Clara County showed that the difficulty of finding a meeting place was a major problem for larger churches. Local planning restrictions, along with the cost of land meant that there was virtually no possibility for a growing church to develop a new complex of buildings for their church life. To further complicate the problem, schools, which would be a logical meeting place, were not generally for hire. These are not unusual conditions in the developed world.

In my experience in church planting, I have known what it means to have to set up chairs and a pulpit, and then try to create an environment where people can come and worship, knowing that at the end of the service, we would take all that down and set up the room in the way it was found. It is time- and energy-consuming. However, these limitations allow for a greater degree of diversity in meeting places. It also creates an environment where the people have a high degree of ownership.

While the small church may be in a better position to solve the problem of where to meet, it is still a difficult issue for many new churches. And there are other problems with single-cell churches. As we have studied them, the first problem is that they have limits to their breadth of ministries. They are not able to provide a variety of age-related or interest-related programmes. They usually have, at best, a small and overwhelmed team of workers. As a result of this limitation, they can stagnate and become inward looking. We have sometimes seen this pattern set in after the first three years.

The most effective way to deal with this problem is to aim for growth through division. Once a church grows to a size of about fifty to eighty people, it should divide itself and plant a new congregation in another area. Of course, in order to do this, it must have been training new leaders from the very beginning.

Another common limitation for the single-cell church is the issue of fear. Small churches can tend to acquire a remnant mentality which hinders the ability to relate to the wider Body of Christ. As a result, they often exclude them-selves from interchurch projects in the community.

To conclude this chapter, I want to underline the remarkable potential of the single-cell church in today's society. There is a powerful and significant potential for increased growth of the Body of Christ through single-cell church planting. It is important that denominational leaders, pastors and church planters understand that only a few highly gifted people will ever be able to establish and lead a large church. However, an average person with a call from God can plant effective single-cell churches. They will need some training and support, but it is not an overwhelming task.

Single-cell churches can also fill a powerful role in meeting the sociological need for family. It is important to understand this need in our society and to seek to meet it by planting single-cell congregations. While the actual size tends to limit the impact that a single-cell congregation can have in a community, we take advantage of the significant power that a group of single-cell congregations could have in a given geographical area. Of course, the co-operation required to make this impact can only happen as the fear of competition is overcome. Perhaps we won't worry about this so much if we concentrate on the many who are still lost. If we take a sober look at our surrounding communities, we will find that usually more than 80 per cent are outside the reach of the Church. If we concentrate on reaching this majority, perhaps we can lay aside our fears and get together with others for celebrations, teaching events and evangelistic outreaches.

If this potential is to be developed, then we must develop effective methodologies for the training and supporting of those who can start new congregations. In Western societies, we tend to develop long-term training programmes that require aspiring leaders to leave their church and become full-time students for several years. But the most effective church planters in the world are being trained in short-term courses where they receive intensive input with immediate implementation, all in a time frame of three to six months.

We need to be creative and provide opportunities for people to become bi-vocationally involved in church planting. To do this, we will need a flexible approach to church, so that, no matter what time they work and what kind of schedule they keep. they can be involved in evangelism and church planting.

Finally, our experience has shown that a powerful and God-given energy is released when people set goals for the multiplication of new congregations. Once such vision is set out by the leadership of a church or a group of churches, God uses that expression of faith to inspire people with a new vision and a desire to get involved. That capacity for vision and involvement will never be explored if the challenge is not issued. It is our conviction that most churches have the potential for growth, but the leader or leaders must first be convinced of that potential. Then they must believe that, if they take such a step towards fulfilling the Great Commission, then God will add his power to their efforts.

PART TWO

BIG VISION –
HOME & AWAY

5

THE PLAN, THE MAN
AND THE CLAN

Then Jesus came to them and said, 'All authority in heaven and on earth has been given to me. Therefore go and make disciples of all nations, baptizing them in the name of the Father and of the Son and of the Holy Spirit, and teaching them to obey everything I have commanded you. And surely I am with you always, to the very end of the age.' Matt 28:18-21

FAMOUS LAST WORDS

The Universal Church has a distinct purpose and mandate, to preach the gospel in all the world. This job, given by Jesus to his church, is not an optional extra, it is not *a* great commission, the good commission or even the great idea. It is *the* Great Commission.

The fact that the Great Commission constitutes the last earthly message of Jesus, given in the aftermath of the shock of the resurrection, gives these instructions an importance that goes beyond that of Jesus' pre-Easter teaching. In his first letter to the Corinthian church, Paul points out that if he preaches he can't boast, it is his obligation. If he does it voluntarily, he is simply discharging the trust committed to him. Yet in a recent survey of British churches, 49 per cent of church leaders agreed with the statement that their church did not go out actively seeking new Christians.

The Great Commission is Jesus' way of engaging his Church in the fulfilment of human destiny – destiny that requires people to progress in two directions, through space and time and in spiritual stature. A full exploration of the mission of the Church would be a book, if not a library in itself, but we do need an understanding of the Church's mission that goes beyond simply convert-making and worship.

In the last chapter we saw the practical importance of the small congregation to the success of this commission. In this chapter we shall examine the Great Commission from a theological perspective that underlines the importance of the local church in God's plan for humanity.

THE PLAN

The Bible is quite clear that the Lord has such a plan. It starts before the beginning of time and concludes in eternity. It starts with a couple commissioned to 'fill up the earth' and ends with people from every tribe, tongue, people and nation praising Jesus. It starts in a garden which contains gold, precious stones and pearl and ends in a city built out of those same raw materials. In the New Testament the Church is presented as integral to this plan.

Paul's letter to the Ephesian church contains some of the richest ideas by which we try to understand God's purpose for creation. In it, he spells out God's intention to join all of his creation to himself. This process was started by the Creator becoming a creature in Jesus and is fulfilled by Jesus' body growing to its full stature (Eph 4:13), at which point all that has not been united in Christ is destroyed. An exact understanding of this union is, as Paul says, a mystery. It is not something we can systematize; it is partially revealed by the allegories the Bible uses for it, such as marriage. The importance of the Church in this mystery is brought out again and again in Ephesians, to the extent that Paul states that even angelic powers hadn't understood the Lord's intentions until the Church emerged (Eph 3:10).

The first chapter of the letter goes to great lengths to convey that salvation in Jesus is not an afterthought aimed at fixing a faulty world made in only six days. Things are the way they are because of certain choices and plans God laid down before the foundation of the world (Eph 1:4-5). In particular, Paul refers to this plan as God's *oikonomia* (Eph 1:10), translated 'plan', 'administration' or 'dispensation'. *Oikonomia* comes from the word for 'house' or 'household' and refers to the plan or arrangements by which a household is managed. From it we get the word 'economics'. Paul then refers to the Church as God's household or *oikeois*, giving us the word 'ecumenical' to refer to the wider Church.

In other words, the mission of the Church is part of God's predetermined plan for creation to reach its predestined fulfilment in a union of creator and creature (Col 1:20). God's purpose for this world is fulfilled by God's plan for his Church, to whom he has entrusted the work of reconciliation (2 Cor 5:17-21). The image of God's 'household economy' being stewarded by the 'household community' adds new depth to many of Jesus' Kingdom parables, which picture God as a returning head of the household settling accounts with his administrators.

The image of the perfect wife being a diligent and shrewd household manager in the last verses of Proverbs is given new meaning when God's purpose of union and reconciliation is depicted in Revelation as a marriage. God's plan for the human race is dependent on his Church being what it is supposed to be and growing to its full stature. His plan needs the whole Church to take the whole gospel to the whole world, and that means that every local church should be actively involved in the Great Commission.

While Ephesians furnishes us with some of the richest and most awe-inspiring understanding of God's purpose for the human race, other parts of scripture give us a clearer picture of God's strategy. In the first chapter of Genesis, we find God creating a world in which his purposes could be achieved.

> Then God said, let us make man in our image, according to our likeness; and let them rule over the fish of the sea and over the birds of the sky and over the cattle and over all the earth, and over every creeping thing that creeps on the earth. And God created man in his own image, in the image of God he created him; male and female he created them. And God blessed them; and said to them, 'Be fruitful and multiply, and fill the earth and subdue it and rule over the fish of the sea and the birds of the sky, and over every living thing that moves on the earth.' Gen 1:26–28

By making humans in his own image, God does what is necessary for his union with us. By making male and female, he gives us an intuitive insight into the way in which two beings that are of like image, but not the same, can become one. (The phrases 'helpmeet' or 'suitable helper' used in Gen 2 to describe the relationship of the woman to the man is used to describe the relationship of God with mankind throughout the rest of the Old Testament).

At the beginning of this century, Sigmund Freud observed that mankind had two driving forces: one was sex and the other was aggression. Both of these 'libido' drives can be seen as a corruption of the instincts that the Lord spoke into human beings' constitution at their creation. God created us to fill up the earth (with more of God's image) and to exercise his delegated authority over it. He wove into our make-up the desires that would ensure that his bride would consist of an innumerable multitude, who together ('them' in Gen 1:26-28) had learnt to steward God's household resources in a worthy and honourable manner.

The corruption of God's primary commission for the human race to Freud's libido forces by people's rebellion highlights the first obstacle to God's intentions. Yet God, in his wisdom, has made that very obstacle a means to his end for creation. However, its immediate consequence is that the image of God in human beings is broken and we are left with no chance of achieving our divine destiny. People are still subject to the drives God gave them to reach the length and breadth, if not the depth, of that destiny. They still feel the desire to propagate and fill up the earth with God's image and they still feel the urge to bring order to it. Just as these desires cannot lead humanity to its destiny in themselves, so they frustrate the individual who looks for fulfilment in sex and power.

Despite the futility to which these created drives have been subjected, the Lord allows them to continue propelling us forward towards their goal of a full and subdued earth. Furthermore, throughout the Old Testament, we continually see God intervening either to restate this objective or hasten progress towards it. The Lord restates this commission to Noah (Gen 9:1-7); he drives mankind out across the face of the earth by confusing their languages at Babel (where people were settling instead of pioneering), and he tells Abraham to 'go forth' and multiply (Gen 12:1-3).

Eventually Jesus expresses these ideas in the Great Commission. The command, 'Go therefore and make disciples of all the nations' restores the ability to fill up the earth with God's image. His statements, ' all authority has been given to me . . .' 'cast out demons, heal the sick, pick up serpents . . .' restore our authority over creation. The broken image has been restored and man is free again to become what he was intended to be.

We have already considered how the revelation of God's image in Jesus and the exercise of his delegated authority are hallmarks of a church. The Church has now become the agent of humanity's destiny. It is the Church that propagates the Lord's image through the earth, both by its corporate revelation and by the process of disciple making. And it is the local congregation that has the immediate commission to administer the authority of God's kingdom in each locale. Putting the Church into this trans-Testamental plan highlights the need for churches to multiply and fill up the earth and to bring in God's kingdom by preaching the whole gospel and exercising spiritual authority locally. As the Church gets on with the Great Commission, God's plan for all of humanity is being realized.

THE MAN

Still further insight into the importance of the Church in this plan can be gained if we consider the pivotal work of Jesus within the same framework which we have sketched above.

Having created human beings with the potential to carry his image and exercise his will over creation, the second stage of God's plan is the preparation for the reconciliation and union of all creation with its creator by the unique synthesis of God and man in Jesus. The preparation for this God-man is the thread that holds the Old Testament together and sets it apart from other writings of that time. The first appearance of God-man is in Genesis 4. Eve's words on giving birth to Cain are literally, 'I have gotten a manchild, the Lord.' Her understanding of God's promise, that her seed would destroy the newly established rule of the serpent, is that God himself would intervene in human history. Like many since, she makes the mistake of expecting the prophecy to be fulfilled instantly.

Perhaps the most succinct statement of what God achieves through the life, death, resurrection and ascension of the God-man, Jesus, is found in Colossians.

> For God was pleased to have all his fullness dwell in him, and through him to reconcile to himself all things, whether things on earth or things in heaven, by making peace through his blood, shed on the cross. Col 1:19-20.

However, we should not think that the work of Jesus was simply to restore things to the way they were before the Fall. Whilst man has been restored, there has been a change in the heart of the Godhead. As expounded elsewhere in the New Testament, God now irrevocably carries the image of man in his own being. Whereas Adam could be joined to God in the way in which a glove is joined to a hand, there is now a mutual interlocking between them, like pieces of a jigsaw. Now the Holy Spirit, which is the Spirit of Jesus and fully human, can couple with a man or woman in such a way as to correct their imperfections without compromising their humanity.

This development is not simply a matter of whim on the Lord's part. John writes in his Gospel that the Holy Spirit had not been given in previous generations, or even to Jesus' contemporaries, because Jesus had not yet been 'glorified', which by John's own standard meant resurrected and ascended. The image of man in the heart of God allows a union of creator and creature which goes beyond anything realized in the Old Testament. Although the Holy Spirit lives in individuals, we have already seen that there is a concentration of the Spirit of Jesus that takes place in the coming together of his people, and this seems to be greater than the sum of its parts. It is also the indwelling presence of the Spirit which is the basis of the Church's unity.

To extend the jigsaw metaphor: God's purpose for humanity is fulfilled by a multidimensional puzzle in which the Father is joined through the work of Jesus by the Holy Spirit to masses of individuals who are themselves joined together as Church by that same Spirit. The Universal Church then extends God's rule by its local expressions exercising their corporate authority throughout the earth.

Whilst the totality of this vision will not be achieved until after Jesus' second coming, the Church is supposed to be making progress towards it, not just sitting and waiting for its imposition. After healing the lame beggar in Acts 3, Peter calls on the crowd to repent so that Jesus can return, 'whom heaven must receive until the period of restoration of all things, about which God spoke . . . from ancient times' (Acts 3:19-21). The gospel message preached by Peter and the response to it are seen as part of the process of bringing Jesus back for the ultimate conclusion of God's plan for humanity.

This joining together of individuals both into and within the Church is fundamental to the reconciliation of all things in Jesus. Paul is clear that this mystery, which represents God's eternal purpose, is only now made known through the Church (Eph 3:9-11). Not only does the Church reveal this reconciling purpose, but it is the corporate people of God who have been entrusted with the work of reconciliation (2 Cor 5:18). This is of course why in the midst of such wonderful eschatology, the book of Ephesians is so concerned with unity – unity of the Church, unity of neighbours, unity of families and unity in marriages.

God's purposes for humanity are only achievable in Jesus, so to find our purpose as individuals we must abide in him. And to abide in Jesus, we must be in relationships of love with our fellow disciples (John 15:4–17). This requires local churches. Just as the original commission to Adam and Eve would have resulted in an extended tribe of families under a single patriarch, so the fulfilment of Jesus' Commission must result in a clan of interrelated communities that cover the earth. Jesus left the accomplishment of a big vision to millions of small churches.

THE CLAN

Every local church carries responsibility for the Great Commission, a big vision that has been beautifully summed up in the vision statement of the AD 2000 and Beyond movement: 'the whole Church taking the whole gospel to the whole world.' But Jesus did not just leave his Church with a huge job to do, he also left it with the framework of a strategy to achieve it. They were to do it in Jerusalem, Judea, Samaria and in the uttermost parts of the earth. Whilst these parameters may seem vague, it tends to be churches that have found the structures and means to express their life at local, regional, national and international levels that are the most effective contributors to the work of the Great Commission. By following this simple strategy, the Church of Jesus Christ has grown from a handful of people to one third of the world's population. According to the 1993 edition of *Operation World*, evangelical Christianity is the only world religion that is growing significantly by conversion. Church history shows us that, whilst God's people have gained and lost ground in different contexts and times, there has been a continuous move forward towards God's ultimate objectives.

The Universal Church is involved in an awe-inspiring task and we can be excited and thrilled by its current success. But this universal Church is made up of local congregations and the most common manifestation of the Church throughout history and throughout the world has been the congregation of less than 120 people. Where bigger churches have emerged, they tend to contain smaller cells within their structure. If the task is ever to be finished, the small church must not fail to work out its missionary mandate because it thinks it has insufficient resources to play its part.

Isaiah and Habakkuk tell us that one day the 'earth will be filled with the knowledge of the glory of the Lord, as the waters cover the sea' (Hab 2:14, Is 11:9). According to Isaiah, this is the immediate precursor to the nations returning to the Messiah. The New Testament is also clear that the knowledge of the invisible God is only found in Jesus: 'If you have seen the Son then you've seen the Father'. We established in Chapter 2 that the revelation of Jesus is one of the things that makes a gathering a church. Putting all this together, it is not unreasonable to assume that the completion of the Great Commission requires a local congregation to be making Jesus known to every person in every distinct community, class, kind and culture, so that everyone has the knowledge of the glory of God even if they don't want to partake in it.

Of course, the small local church will need to focus its

understanding of God's plan down to a more human scale. It cannot be fully committed all of the time to everything that world mission implies. Jesus' plan is workable because it allows for progressive involvement. A local church's first priority is to take the whole gospel to its particular locality or cultural grouping, its 'Jerusalem'. There is then a responsibility to 'network' with other nearby churches to bring the whole gospel to a wider region or even a nation, their 'Judea and Samaria'. And finally, a congregation may play a specific role in a particular outpost of the world.

A local church starts reaching all the world by defining its local target community and fully preaching the gospel to it. Throughout the New Testament, we continually find the word 'church' qualified in a way which indicates its missionary context, it is 'the church of the Gentiles', 'the church in Rome' or 'the church throughout Judea, Galilee and Samaria'. A missionary congregation has as acute an understanding of what it means to be, for example, the Church in Bognor as it does to be an Evangelical Baptist Church.

If a church defines its 'Jerusalem' geographically, there may be sub-communities within the territory that they will need help in reaching or will need to join with other congregations to reach. Today, most of the world's population lives in cities. Whereas village communities are usually made up of one cultural grouping, cities confuse the issue. Paul would use Gentile forums to reach the Gentile people in a city and synagogues to reach Jews. Today's cities are far more complex than the ones Paul worked in, with modern transport, communications, work patterns and religious and ethnic diversity creating an incredible tangle of subcultures, classes, kinds and networks of people all living in the same geography. The reality of today's cities requires a host of congregations to reach all distinct strata and locales.

Defining a church's local target community will help it to be more focused in its efforts to reach the wider region or nation and the uttermost ends of the earth. Instead of sending out missionaries willy-nilly, successful missionary congregations identify the niche into which they will put the majority of their resources. This focus allows a congregation to develop a working knowledge and relationship with a particular language group, nation or city. It enables more of its members to play an active part in its evangelization through prayer, short-term visits, resource collection, and so on.

Defining a local church's 'Jerusalem', 'Judea', 'Samaria' are important steps towards its understanding itself in relation to the whole church and the whole world. Having defined these different spheres of operation, it still remains for the local congregation to take the whole gospel to these respective communities.

THE WHOLE GOSPEL

God's purpose for humanity is huge, and that purpose is accomplished by the spreading and multiplication of churches through a big territory – all the earth (Matt 24:14, 28:19, Mark 16:15). Congregations both accomplish this spread and maintain their purpose by taking the 'whole gospel'. It should not come as a surprise that the gospel is as deep as the vision is wide. We have already thought about this depth in terms of our union with God. It should be obvious that such depth cannot be reduced to a single methodology or technique.

Soon, anyone will be able to turn on a radio anywhere in the world and 'hear the gospel' in the relevant language. However, reaching this admirable goal does not signal the accomplishment of 'preach the gospel in all the world and then the end will come'. At the heart of God is relationship, Father, Son and Holy Spirit. At the heart of the good news is relationship, the reconciliation of God and humanity, the marriage of Christ and his bride, the destruction of divisions like Jew and Gentile. So it is not unreasonable to assume that relationship is also fundamental to the preaching of the gospel.

John effectively starts his Gospel by saying that Jesus didn't just bring a message, he *was* the message: 'In the beginning was the Word . . .' Making the gospel known is not just a matter of speaking words, the words need to be made flesh to those that are hearing them. The message is essential – without it, all that Jesus was is open to specula-tion. But in Jesus we see the messenger being inextricably tied to the message.

In this light, the role of the local church is paramount to the preaching of the gospel. As the body of Christ, it is the place where the Word becomes flesh, a living demonstration of the loving purposes of the Father. As a local church starts to think about how it can play its part in God's strategy, it must come to terms with the fact that taking the whole gospel means far more than publicly reciting some of the post-Easter creeds found in Paul's letters (1 Cor 15:1-4).

To quote one commentator, the death and resurrection of Jesus are 'the centre of the gospel, but not its circumfer-ence'. A local church wanting to play its part in missions must first learn to embody the whole gospel in its imme-diate context. Standing firmly on the foundation of the cross, a church starts engaging in mission by encompassing those around them within the broader horizons of the gospel – its social concern and the supernatural love of God.

The early church seems to have seen the job of pro-claiming the gospel as a continuation of the ministry of

Jesus. Luke starts the book of Acts by explaining that his gospel was an account of 'all that Jesus *began* to do and teach until the day he was taken up to heaven, after giving instructions . . . to the apostles'. If Jesus' earthly life, as recorded in Luke, constitutes the beginning of Jesus' ministry, then the Acts of his body (the Church) represent its continuing ministry. This is a clear statement of the continuity between the ministry of Jesus and the continuing work of the Church.

Jesus viewed his work as including proclamation, power and philanthropy. In Luke 4, Jesus uses the book of Isaiah to introduce the work he has come to do: 'The Spirit of the Lord is upon me, because He anointed me to preach the Gospel to the poor. He has sent me . . .' Jesus claims that he is both anointed and sent to preach the gospel, this includes 'to proclaim release to the captives . . . and set free the downtrodden' (philanthropy – social concern) '. . . recovery of sight to the blind' (power - supernatural), '. . . to proclaim the favourable year of the Lord' (proclamation – preaching). In the three years that followed, Jesus preached about God's Kingdom, healed the sick and carried a purse for the poor.

In Rom 15:17-18, Paul states that he too has used words, works and wonders to 'fully preach the gospel of Christ' from Jerusalem to Illyricum. And in Acts 3 and 4, we find the newly formed church also involved in healing, preaching and social action (see Acts 3:2f, 4:8f, 4:34).

Since New Testament times, local churches have been involved in all three of these areas of ministry. Unfortunately, one is often emphasized at the expense of the other two. It has been well argued that, since there are other agencies that will heal the sick and tackle social injustice, the Church should make its primary focus the preaching of the message. But, if we preach a gospel of love and a God who loves, then our message only has credibility if we ourselves live in this truth, if we express our love in practical terms and if God's love is demonstrated by his supernatural intervention. Loving is not something that we can do in isolation. it requires community and this brings us back to the role of the Church in the preaching of the whole gospel. Local churches are the place where the words become flesh.

A missionary congregation knows its mission field and this knowledge opens up the possibility of ministering to its needs in a way that creates channels for the love of God to touch and heal lives. As with Jesus, a church may heal ten to see only one respond to the Lord, they may feed 5000 to be deserted by all but a few, but they have been faithful in preaching the whole gospel. A local congregation begins its role in mission by incarnating the whole ministry of Jesus to the community around them.

CONCLUSIONS

In the last chapter, we thought about the practical success of the local church and its need to reach various communities. In this chapter we have considered the importance of the Church in God's cosmic plan and how this relates to the local Church and we have considered the depth of the gospel the Church is supposed to preach. In the next few chapters we will attempt to fill out these grand principles with specific illustrations, practical ideas, comments, observations and teaching which are directly relevant to the small local church.

6

PARTNERSHIP AT HOME

In John 13:35, Jesus tells his disciples, 'by this all men will know that you are my disciples, if you love one another.' In recent years, many evangelistic initiatives have successfully used public opinion polls as part of their programme. The results of such polls, along with the experience of Christians engaged in personal evangelism, reveal a prevailing attitude toward Christianity. The majority of people in the UK and many other Western nations still believe that Jesus Christ is the Son of God and the Bible is the Word of God, but they have no wish to become involved with organized religion. If you were to ask why, most people would cite one or more reasons why they dislike church. One of those reasons would go something like this: 'There are so many different kinds of churches, and they each say they are right and all the others are wrong.'

This attitude, which is the most common excuse for not being involved in church life, seems to prove that the converse of Jesus' statement is also true: 'that all men will doubt that you are my disciples, if you do not love one another.' In this chapter, several practical ways for churches to work together with other churches and some ideas for building and strengthening genuine unity are presented.

It is important to acknowledge that unity between believers is a commanded state of affairs. Anything short of that is disobedience to the commandments of Jesus. No serious Christian would argue against the importance of unity. We all believe in the truth of the words of Jesus in John 13:35. And yet, many churches remain completely isolated from other churches in their area. This seems to be a contradiction in terms, but any Christian leader will know exactly why this state of affairs exists: we agree that unity is important, but we disagree about the grounds for unity.

Books could be and have been written on the subject of unity. Indeed, the outworking of our unity can get complicated and often requires much wisdom and access to the experience of others. Yet the grounds for our unity are not very complicated. The apostle Paul writes in Eph 4:3-6: 'Make every effort to keep the unity of the Spirit through the bond of peace. There is one body and one Spirit – just as you were called to one hope when you were called – one Lord, one faith, one baptism; one God and Father of all, who is over all and through all and in all.' Note that our unity is a unity of Spirit, not of mind.

Everyone who knows and loves the Lord Jesus Christ does so for only one reason: they have been born of the Spirit. This unity of the Spirit forms a bond between all who are born of the Spirit; Paul calls it the bond of peace. So, all believers start from a place of unity, but we can either strengthen or damage the bonds that tie us together. When we introduce any additional grounds for unity, we run the risk of damaging or destroying that unity.

This biblical approach to unity is actually quite foreign to the way our minds work in Western nations today. Many recent writers have pointed out that we, in the West, have inherited more of a Greek way of thinking than a Judaic way of thinking. One of the results of this Greek inheritance is that we exalt logic and reason. When it comes to unity, we tend to base our unity on mental agreement. We often draw up battle lines and fight over concepts, doctrines and ideas. As important as these matters might be, they are not the grounds on which our unity is based.

In Eph 4, Paul goes on to write, '. . . so the body of Christ may be built up until we all reach unity in the faith and in the knowledge of the Son of God and become mature . . .' From this passage, we can infer that there is a need for us to grow in a common understanding. However, a common understanding is not our starting point. When Paul sets out the unity of the Spirit as the starting point, he gives us a framework for staying in unity while we work on our differences of understanding.

There seems to be no biblical basis for a person or congregation to withdraw from fellowship with other persons or congregations because of differences of opinion. If the leadership and members of another congregation claim Jesus as their Lord and Saviour, then we are commanded to maintain the unity that already exists between us by virtue of the fact that we are all born of the same Spirit.

In addition to the biblical imperative to maintain unity, there is a simple practical factor: small churches that isolate themselves from others in the Body of Christ rarely thrive. The Father designed the Church so that we need one another.

In light of the imperative and practical need for unity, how does a leader of a congregation begin to build unity with other churches in the area? Sometimes such efforts fail because one party or another expects too much too soon. Unity is strengthened one step at a time.

What we are advocating is that unity between local congregations should be strong enough to support partnerships in public activities. Such unity cannot be developed and sustained by public activities alone; it normally first requires regular personal contact between leaders. Both authors are involved with a number of interchurch or inter-denominational activities, and the best of them are built on friendships which have been developed and strengthened over time. These friendships might emerge from Churches Together structure, a minister's fraternal meeting, or they might first develop around some event. Billy Graham, Luis Palau and other evangelists of international repute have made multi-faceted contributions to church life in the UK, but perhaps their greatest contribution has been in the shape of stronger interchurch unity. Their church leaders' meeting often provided a most effective forum for unity to begin to grow. In hundreds of towns and cities, these leaders meetings have continued on a regular basis long after the event was concluded.

In some cases, though, even these kinds of settings can seem to demand too much too soon. There is really no substitute for personal contact with a view to developing friendship. Now the idea of approaching another minister or leader of a congregation could well be a little threatening, but someone must bridge the gap. And there is no doubt that the benefits of greater unity in the Body of Christ make it worth a little risk.

In many parts of Britain, friendship initiatives between leaders have resulted in partnership activities which have in turn led to significant church growth. Several years ago in north London, a small group of ministers and leaders of fellowships began to meet together. At the outset, they had no plans to do anything other than fellowship together, but the fellowship grew deeper and more meaningful for each of them. Now, after several years of deepening friendship, they regularly speak in one another's pulpits, hold joint services for all their churches and invite major, international speakers for the benefit of the whole city.

This sort of fellowship between church leaders is definitely on the increase. Even though it takes precious time to participate in such a group, most leaders who do so would say that the mutual support of the group and the sense of greater blessing on their work certainly makes it worth it. Prayer for one another has become the main feature of many of these groups and for many leaders, they have found that it is the one place where they can be completely open and be understood and prayed for. Even pastors need to be pastored. Or perhaps we should say pastors especially need to be pastored.

Once fellowship between leaders begins to grow, then there is a good foundation for public unity. Public unity can be expressed in many different ways: pulpit exchanges, interchurch celebrations, co-operative evangelistic events or ongoing strategies like March for Jesus or DAWN.

March for Jesus has often proved to be an ideal opportunity for the first steps of publicly expressed unity. March for Jesus has sought to draw believers together on grounds that are common to all believers. Even though people of many different theological persuasions participate, they come together under the simple banner of the Lordship of Jesus Christ. The non-controversial nature of the theme of March for Jesus, along with the simplicity of the event itself, makes it a good vehicle for the first steps of public unity in a village, town or city.

The DAWN strategy provides a very good framework for ongoing unity and co-operation. There are several good reasons why it has proven to be so effective in many nations. Probably the greatest reasons for its success is the fact that it draws leaders and their churches together for the right reason. Its aim is regularly to reach every person with the gospel. That is a purpose which is bound to enjoy God's blessing.

Another of its strengths is that it affirms the difference

between denominations and between individual congregations. Therefore, it does not advocate a particular kind of churchmanship or evangelistic strategy. Rather, it encourages each congregation to seek to multiply after its own kind. Often, churches find it difficult to participate in interchurch evangelistic initiatives, because they represent such a major diversion of time and other precious resources. Often, smaller churches are aware that they might invest much and then receive few converts from the evangelistic events. The larger churches always seem to have a greater profile in such interchurch events.

DAWN, on the other hand, encourages church leaders to meet together, pray together and lead their congregations to pray together for their city. But the end goal is that each church might multiply after its own kind. Through regular fellowship together, the leaders of churches can avoid unhelpful overlap while assuring that every neighbourhood in their town or city is being targeted with the gospel.

One of the best publicized local expressions of the DAWN strategy has been the SHINE initative at St Helens. SHINE stands for St Helens Interchurch Neighbourhood Evangelization. After a year of co-operative research and consultation, a significant part of the whole church in St Helens committed themselves to working together to make theirs a Christ-centred town. In June 1992, their goals to plant thirty new churches and raise the church-going percentage of the population to 20 per cent by the end of the decade were presented at an open-air rally attended by two bishops and the Free Church Moderator for the area. No church had been planted in St Helens for over thirty years and the church-planting goal was divided into two-year sub-goals to make it a realistic proposition. The churches of St Helens seem to be on target for their goal of three new churches by the end of 1994. However, more interestingly, before any new churches were planted, it was discovered that churches involved with SHINE grew an average of 10 per cent each in the year after their public commitment to work together. Phil Pawley, SHINE's co-ordinator, put the growth down to three factors: an increased sense of purpose in church members, the benefits of their joint prayer strategy for the town and increased blessing on their attempts at unity.

Of course the possibilities for partnership extend beyond other churches in your area. The Church consists of many groups, organizations and associations with specialist expertise. Specialist areas of ministries are often the key to getting the gospel message to receptive people. Your church may have no idea how to reach out to an ethnic minority group in your neighbourhood, but a team from YWAM or Operation Mobilization or any number of mission organizations could be just what you need!

Perhaps you or someone in your congregation have identified a group of people with special needs who might have indicated a responsiveness to the gospel. That group might be mothers with toddlers, it might be young couples who want help to strengthen their marriage or it might even be a group requiring a high level of specialization, such as people with AIDS or pregnant women who need to be presented with an alternative to abortion. In each of these cases and in many others, there are ministries that specialize in meeting these needs within the context of Christian outreach.

People with deeply felt personal needs are often the most open to change and therefore the ones most likely to be open to the gospel. I once met a young woman who had a wonderful testimony of how Christ had set her free from anorexia. She and the counsellor who had helped her to freedom felt that they could share with others some of the things they had learnt and that this would provide an opportunity to convey the good news to others. After prayer, they developed a strategy for reaching people with eating disorders. Working under the auspices of their local church, they put up posters at supermarkets and other food outlets. Then they distributed flyers with registration forms to shoppers. To their astonishment, they had to move the first meeting from the church to the town hall because they had nearly 400 participants.

Few small churches feel that they possess the required expertise to meet specialist needs, but a partnership with another part of the Body of Christ could well provide the missing abilities. Many of those groups that possess specialist knowledge and abilities have recognized that their best use of resources is to train the members of churches. Such specialist ministries must aim to impart their knowledge and abilities to local congregations. If they pursue their ministries in such a way that they do not make an enriching contribution to the life of local congregations, then they will have failed to make the most of their calling.

The Holy Spirit strongly blesses partnership efforts and projects. He does so because partnership is one of the ways that we help the Body of Christ to work in the way it was designed to. Partnership also enables believers to widen their network of relationships, thus increasing the 'bonds of peace' within one Body. And 'by this all men will know that you are my disciples, if you love one another.'

Of course, partnership, co-operation and unity are lovely concepts, but a messy reality. You get a hint of the messiness in Psalm 133, which is a song about how good unity is. So good, in fact, is unity that it is likened to oil running down Aaron's beard, which would no doubt mess up Aaron's clothes – the most luxurious designer ensemble in all Jerusalem. Of course, the oil may be messy, but it represented the priestly anointing. The implication of this Psalm is that the anointing to mediate between God and humanity is released by our harmony. However we might expect it to be manifest, there are very few churches that do not want more anointing.

Sadly it is not always true that the biggest and most vibrant local churches are also most gracious and non-divisive. It is often the case that size and success bring a little pride into a congregation, and this can cause a degree of slackness when it comes to preserving the bond of peace. Certainly, Stockbrook Christian Fellowship can not be said to be the 'biggest and best' local church in Derby. Yet their openness and commitment to the whole church of the city has allowed them to initiate projects and programmes which go way beyond their own meagre resources.

Stockbrook Christian Fellowship was planted in 1986 out of a Baptist house group and a Youth for Christ team. Eleven adults and nine children moved from all points of the compass into a poorly churched neighbourhood. This co-operation between congregation and mission agency at Stockbrook's inception set a course that has served them well in the years following.

Stockbrook's vision was to present a gospel that included words, works and wonders (as outlined in Chapter 5) to a particular part of Derby, a city in the English Midlands. An extensive evangelism programme was started, which included social action, an education project, door-to-door calling, tent missions, barbecues and mother and toddler clubs. In the course of their evangelism, Stockbrook Christian Fellowship had the pleasure of seeing some of their new contacts healed both physically and emotionally. By 1990, the church had grown to over eighty adults and thirty or more children.

During this period, Stockbrook Christian Fellowship

started to explore ways of partnering with the local community and other community organizations to open up new points of contact with their neighbours and to give them access to greater resources. In 1988, a member of the congregation, Carl Taylor, started a social action project called Third Wave, designed to reach those marginalized in society, the long-term unemployed, the house-bound, single parents and other disadvantaged groups. Funding was obtained from the city council and the Manpower Services Commission to carry out an audit of 2500 people, half of whom indicated they would like further contact with the project. As a result of the audit, Third Wave decided to set up an advice and guidance centre. A grant was obtained from the government and a centre was started which was to work closely with the council, the Careers Service and Evangelical Enterprise.

During this time, Stockbrook Christian Fellowship had also been developing links with other churches in the city and with a number of Christian organizations. During 1990, Stockbrook held a mission which drew on the experience and resources of Youth With A Mission, Operation Mobilization and the Icthtus Christian Fellowship in London. They also organized transport for Derby churches to take part in the regional March for Jesus in 1990 and 1992 and organized a local march for eleven churches in 1991.

In 1990, Third Wave expanded to provide practical project teams for disadvantaged people in painting, decorating and gardening, acting as a subcontractor for other providers of training locally. While Third Wave grew, the church itself faced its first setback with the failure of a church plant and the loss of a couple of leaders. In 1991, it had declined to sixty adults and twenty or so children, and most of the leadership now fell on to a single couple, Phil and Gill Sharples.

Under Carl Taylor's oversight, Third Wave was growing and growing; by 1992, it was involved in over 400 projects a year and was taking referrals from the Citizens Advice Bureau, the Health Authority, the government's Business Sector and the Enterprise Council. Its advice and guidance work now covered debt, welfare rights and signposting to other specialist advice services. The church had also developed links with local primary schools through a regular pantomime, written and performed by members of the church each Christmas.

The church found itself in a place of seemingly limitless contact with the community, but desperate for the spiritual fellowship that would enable it to capitalize on this opportunity. Phil Sharples decided to strengthen his contacts with other churches, in particular his links with the Ichthus Christian Fellowship in London and with Derby Asian Fellowship. As a result, the two Derby churches went away together to a family camp organized by the Ichthus Christian Fellowship.

For Stockbrook Christian Fellowship, 1992 proved to be a pivotal year. Attending the English DAWN congress in Birmingham had convinced Phil that the church needed both to refocus its vision and help to catalyse a strategy of evangelism and church planting for the city. The formation of a ministers' fraternal, called Vision For Derby, provided Phil with the ideal forum to start sharing some of his dreams and ideas. However, the process of refocusing the church's vision and purpose and developing and training a new leadership structure resulted in a number of families leaving the church, and the church now had just fifty adults and children as its core membership.

In the last couple of years, Phil has been able to use his relationships with other churches in the city to introduce the beginnings of a co-operative city-wide evangelism and church planting strategy. Eighty church leaders from over forty churches across the city came together for the first day consultation on such a strategy in 1994. Further consultations are planned, and there was a recognition of the importance of a number of local co-operative initiatives. On Fire, the JIM Challenge, an Operation Mobilization mission and a YWAM mission to the city are planned for 1995. The strong resource and administrative centre that Third Wave has become played its part in facilitating or organizing all these events in some way.

Stockbrook Christian Fellowship now has a leadership team of seven and is receiving regular input from the Ichthus Christian Fellowship to help build it up in strength and size so that it can realize its own local vision as well as facilitate the wider Body of Christ in the city.

There is a story about John Wesley that states that on one occasion while riding to his next campaign he realized he hadn't encountered any opposition to his work for some time. Concerned that he must be losing his spiritual edge he raised the matter with the Lord. At that moment he was hit by a stone thrown by a pedestrian who had just recognized him. Wesley greeted the projectile with a smile and a 'praise the Lord'. Involvement in missions always brings opposition and spiritual attack.

Stockbrook Christian Fellowship's experiences as a small church with a big vision have not always been pleasant, but Phil has not let their vision be reduced to the size of the church. There is no easy route to missionary success for a local congregation, yet without being involved in missions, a local church loses its purpose. In countless surveys, the most commonly given given reason for the absence from church of those that call themselves Christians, is that church seems irrelevant. This lack of relevance might be more than just a cultural issue. It might represent the spiritual reality of many local churches that have missed the point of their existence and have simply become sanctified Rotary Clubs.

Stockbrook Christian Fellowship has defined its 'Jerusalem' and sought to take the whole gospel to its corner of Derby. It has played its part in its 'Judea' by using its resources to facilitate all sorts of evangelism across the city. In terms of 'Samaria', it has joined a number of national initiatives, being regular organizers of the March for Jesus and introducing DAWN to Vision for Derby. At home, it has played its part to the best of its abilities in the Great Commission.

7

PARTNERSHIP AWAY

As each of us labours in our own corner of 'God's vineyard', it is easy to lose sight of an extraordinary fact: the growth of the Church of Jesus Christ in the past twenty-five years is the largest people movement (non-political or non-military) in the earth's history. For every evangelical Christian in 1970 there were about fifteen people who had never heard the gospel. By 1994, that number had been reduced to only six. This figure reflects the fact that the Church round the world has been growing dramatically. Meanwhile, believers have been reaching more and more people who were previously beyond the sound of the gospel.

This growth is due, in part, to the mobilization of the Church in the two-thirds world. As recently as 1950, the number of missionaries from first-world nations like the UK and the USA dwarfed any missionary efforts from poorer nations. That has changed in a most dramatic fashion in recent years. Some time around the start of the 1990s, the number of cross-cultural missionaries from the two-thirds world surpassed the number of missionaries from the first world.

This momentum from two-thirds world nations has had a dramatic effect on our efforts to complete the Great Commission. In so many instances, these new missionaries successfully integrate with people groups who have been very difficult for Westerners to penetrate. Scores of examples could be cited, but here are just two. In Albania, some of the most fruitful church planters are Brazilians. There are many observable reasons for their success, including their joyful and uncomplicated approach to the gospel and church life. They also have the 'advantage' of being poor. Because of currency difficulties and the relative poverty of the churches that send them, they don't have enough money to acquire many of the comforts and conveniences which European and American missionaries usually possess. While most Western missionaries have to be concerned with security for their vehicles, houses and other belongings, the Brazilians live amongst the Albanians. This, in turn, makes it easier for them to plant appropriate churches.

The Turkic people of Turkey and the central Asian countries have a language and culture that are difficult for English speakers and other northern Europeans. During recent years, though, an increasing number of Korean Christians have successfully learned Turkish or the other related languages and have begun to bear fruit amongst these Muslim peoples. This is partly due to the fact that the language and culture of Korea are related to those of the Turkic peoples. A Korean worker in Turkey recently told me, 'English is very hard for me. But when I speak Turkish, it fits me. The structure of the language enables me to express who I am; just like Korean.' There are tens of thousands of good news stories like the two mentioned above.

As exciting as this mobilization of the two-thirds world church is, there is another dimension of equal or greater importance: local churches are getting more directly and fully involved in missions than ever before. For the past 200 years of Protestant Church history, the task of world evangelization has largely been the domain of mission agencies. Local churches usually expressed their involvement, if at all, by sending money and occasionally by sending a person. But most congregations did not send people and relatively few made giving to missions a high priority. Only about 5 per cent of Christian giving is directed into foreign missions.

Perhaps mission agencies contributed to the poor state of affairs by accepting this implied élitism. In some ways, they strengthened the argument for their right to exist by stressing the expertise required in cross-cultural missions. It was too complicated for churches to try it, but as long as the churches would send people and money, they would get on with the task of the Great Commission. No one would have openly taught that the task of world missions was limited to a highly committed élite corps of missionaries, but that message was clearly implied.

There are some obvious weaknesses in this state of affairs. Firstly, we all understand that, in spite of great progress, the completion of the Great Commission is a huge task. It will require the obedient participation of the whole Church of Jesus Christ. Secondly, whereas missionaries and mission teams from the apostle Paul onwards have planted hundreds of thousands of churches, the greatest force for multiplication within the Kingdom of God starts functioning when churches plant churches.

We do not wish to enter into the arguments about the comparative merit of mission agencies or local church-based efforts. Both are legitimate expressions of the Church and the full contributions of all resources will be required in the task of reaching 'every creature'. But both local churches and mission agencies have sometimes found it more comfortable to keep missions separate from the responsibilities of local churches. Thankfully, this false line of demarcation is being rubbed out and churches everywhere are engaging them-selves in the task of reaching the whole world.

At first glance, it would appear that larger churches have a definite advantage over small churches when it comes to direct missions involvement. They more often have the people, the money, the influence, the international contacts which make it almost easy to get involved in cross-cultural mission efforts. Attendance on a Sunday at Kensington Temple, the large Elim Pentecostal Church in London, illustrates this point. Their bulletin board is covered with photos of their own church missionaries. The congregation is composed of people from literally scores of nations from Algeria to Zambia and so they have relational links into scores of nations. Through these links, they continually send more missionaries to plant new churches and influence existing churches and denominations in many nations. They have a full-time training course that prepares more of their members for evangelism and mission work. Their minister and other members of their leadership team travel abroad regularly as they conduct evangelistic outreaches on other continents. Their missions' pastor recently told us that one of his goals is to have each one of their three or four thousand members participate in a short-term team abroad. Now that is a missionary church!

Such a church has, in effect, developed its own full-fledged mission agency. It has sufficient resources and experience to enable it to sustain a credible, fruitful mission programme. That is not to say that it doesn't need to partner with other churches and mission agencies. In the case of Kensington Temple, the leadership team are always on the look-out for fruitful partnerships, but speaking in the purely natural terms of resources and ability, they could sustain their own self-sufficient mission programme.

This kind of programme is clearly well beyond the reach of a small church. Does this mean, therefore, that the small church is unable to participate in missions beyond the occasional missionary visit or offering? Of course not! The commandment to go into all the world and preach the gospel was given to the whole church, so the whole church must be able to participate.

We are writing from a very strong pro-missions position here, and it might be best if we state why. We are convinced that when we obey the commandments of Jesus and do the work that he gave us to do, then he is with us most powerfully. It is our conviction that the Church, and every congregation of it, will thrive and know the anointing of the Spirit most powerfully in all dimensions when it is committed to obey all the commandments of Jesus. It is not uncommon for congregational leadership to take a good, long look at the people they are leading and conclude, 'We can't be involved in mission until we have our own house in order.' We are convinced that this is inevitably a one-way road to greater weakness. The Kingdom of God turns the wisdom of man on its head. 'Give and it shall be given unto you.' 'When I am weak, then I am strong.' 'It is not by might nor by power, but by my Spirit.' Sacrificial commitment to the Great Commission is one of the keys to releasing the grace and power of God into any local church.

Since a small church does not have the resources to mount its own complete mission movement, it must seek partners with whom it can work. Partners in mission can be found in other larger churches, in coalitions of churches or in mission agencies. Partnership programmes can also come in a variety of shapes and sizes. Think back to the example of Henley Baptist Church in Chapter 1. The great majority of their regular attenders (about 100) are involved in some dimension of outreach to Kazakhstan. Kazakhstan is a frontier missions situation. That is, they are working amongst a people who have no indigenous church. Though there are Russian-speaking churches, there was no Kazakh church in the Shymkent region before Henley Baptist became involved. We stress this point because some missiologists would still perpetuate a measure of élitism by claiming that though churches might undertake some efforts in missions, they cannot take on all the challenges of frontier missions.

There was a definite progression of attitudes and events that led to Henley Baptist's mission outreach to the people of Shymkent. It is important to understand something of the progression because it helps to break down an intimidating idea into small steps, each of which is within the realm of the possible. It all started, predictably, within the heart of the senior leader, Frank Payne. God began to challenge him to broaden his vision beyond the size and health of his own congregation. He began to be convinced of the fact that the size and growth of his own church was far too important to him. It had become a symbol of success and status . He was determined to be a successful pastor, which meant pro-ducing a large congregation. But the Lord wanted him to have other priorities. When he acknowledged that those were not right attitudes, the Lord began to challenge him about being committed to the whole Kingdom of God, not just the one congregation.

Through the DAWN Congress in 1992, Frank began to experience a renewal of vision for missions. At this point, though, he couldn't imagine what he and his small church could do. This can often be a frustrating period for a church leader. He or she wants to get involved more widely but can't see how that is possible or what they might have to offer. This is the time for prayer.

If we know the importance of mission and want to be involved, then God will make a way. The time between willingness and actual involvement is an important time for prayer and preparation. Once the members of the congregation are convinced that they ought to be involved, then they should look for opportunities and pray that God will guide them. In Frank's case, the church found the pathway into cross-cultural missions through his attendance at a conference. It was there that he met Misha Grigoriyan and the doors began to open. God works that way. As we get on with the ministry he has called us to, he will open new doors of opportunity.

It was also very significant that the doors opened as Frank was exercising his strongest spiritual gift, being a pastor. As he got alongside Misha as a friend and was willing to strengthen and encourage Misha, a door into Kazakhstan opened. Again, the progression seemed quite normal and natural.

A church and its leadership do not have to master some vast body of knowledge before they get involved in cross-cultural missions. All of the gifts and abilities that are needed in the local church are also needed in missions. A pastor or teacher or administrator who makes a valuable contribution in a local congregation will also have something to give in a missions setting. The converse is also true. Those who have little or nothing to contribute into the life of the local congregation will probably not bear much fruit in a missions setting.

We do not imply that cross-cultural missions, and especially frontier missions, is much the same as working within one's own people. There is a great deal to be learned, and that is one of the areas in which partnership can be so valuable. A small church can enter into a joint effort with partners who have more experience. But so much can be learned by doing. It is our experience that those who are humble and teachable, those who know they have much to learn and do not assume that their own ethnic and cultural background is superior, learn quickly. They will make mistakes, but those mistakes are usually readily forgiven by their hosts if they are humble and teachable.

Once Frank had made a couple of trips to Kazakhstan, he knew that he could not make the most of the opportunities that were being put before him. The regional government wanted help in business. Henley Baptist had two businessmen who, after their first trip, were deeply committed to helping the people of Kazakhstan, but there was a need for scores of business initiatives as well as a wide range of teaching on Christian principles in business. The government was also requesting dozens of English teachers, but the congregation would do well to provide two.

Frank had already called on his Baptist links and, to some extent on his links with Salt and Light, the network of new churches. These were providing the likelihood of some long-term help, but not enough to maintain credibility with the government of Shymkent, and certainly not enough to take advantage of the marvellous opportunity to reach out to an unreached nation. At that point, he contacted the mission agency he knew best, YWAM. After a trip to Shymkent, Kazakhstan, the YWAM leadership and Frank agreed that they could pursue a partnership project together. The trip together was essential because it gave them time to discover whether or not they had sufficient agreement on the basic ingredients of the project. When they had completed a week of travelling together, they knew that they shared in common the three essential ingredients of a partnership of this kind: common goals, common methods of ministry and strong mutual respect.

These are the most important aspects of a partnership initiative. If any of them is missing, conflict will follow. It is always worth the considerable time it takes to discuss these things through in some depth and preferably on location.

Once this much common ground has been covered, then an appropriate organizational and legal framework must be established. In the case of the Shymkent project, the leaders of YWAM and the Henley Baptist initiative had to decide whether this project would be pursued under the legal and financial umbrella of YWAM, Henley Baptist Church or some third alternative. The legal framework of a local Baptist church was not adequate for such an undertaking, but the name YWAM wasn't the best either, because 'mission' is a term which arouses misunderstandings and fears in Kazakhstan.

Finding an appropriate legal and organizational structure for a partnership is of vital importance. Questions of identity, ownership and authority over financial affairs are bound to arise and need to be settled at the beginning of any undertaking with partners. In this case, Frank and the two businessmen from his church had already begun to set up a simple trust under which the project could operate. The YWAM people looked at the nature of the trust and stated that they were very happy to work under the identity and authority of the trust, while Frank invited a couple of YWAM personnel to become trustees.

We have taken the time and space to go into this project in some depth because it contains so many of the most common ingredients of a good, workable partnership project. But it is just one of many examples of small churches getting involved in partnership projects with mission agencies. It is our conviction that this sort of endeavour will become more and more common in the future. We believe, in fact, that mission agencies who are not willing to sacrifice their solo identity for partnership activities will be stuck in the past. We will briefly come back to that subject a little later, but first we want to point out that there are other good models of partnership abroad.

Bethany Fellowship in Hertfordshire has already planted a second congregation in their home town, Harpenden. But they haven't stopped there. They have become a partner church in East, West Ministries. Ron Hibbet, who heads up East, West Ministries, is an Assemblies of God minister, but he has drawn together churches from other backgrounds too. Through his coalition of local churches, Bethany, an independent fellowship, has become deeply involved in the various parts of what used to be Yugoslavia. Though they are a small congregation, they have developed a very broad ministry to and through the churches in that war-torn region.

The leaders of Bethany began by visiting various churches in Serbia and Macedonia but soon broadened their activities to include training emerging church planters and church leaders, sponsoring leaders through Bible training courses, hosting those same leaders for a period of exposure to church life in England, taking lorry-loads of aid and even pleading the cause, at government level, of the suffering people throughout the region. Their extensive efforts have gained the attention and assistance of much of their home town and surrounding area.

Like the project in Kazakhstan, this is not a simple undertaking; it is a significant frontier missions effort and so requires an appropriate legal structure, cross-cultural expertise, financial strength and a broad range of ministry gifts. It is highly unlikely that any single small church could successfully mount an operation of this nature, but when they form a coalition under capable leadership, they become an effective part of the work force in cross-cultural mission.

These are two types of more structured, formal partnerships. That is not to say that they are not highly relational. But the framework in which they work together has been thought through carefully and committed to a legal and financial structure for partnership. There are, undoubtedly, many other types of partnerships into which small churches can enter. But not all of them need to be formal and structured.

At this point, it would be best if one of the authors, as a leader of a mission agency, briefly addressed the reader:

I am delighted to see the growing fellowship, co-operation and partnership opportunities between local churches and organizations. There have been times when considerable defensiveness coloured and strained the relationships between mission agencies and many local churches. It appears that that tension has been on the wane for several years now, and in its place has come a growing sense of mutual commitment to both strengthening congregations and reaching unreached peoples. Recent communication and fellowship with the minister of a local church serve to illustrate this.

This minister's small congregation has sent one of their finest young people to an Eastern European country via our mission agency. They have not been able to provide him full financial support, but there is no doubt about their commitment to him. They have prayed for him and helped him in every way possible and God has provided the extra money he has needed.

Part of the care that the church has extended has been an occasional pastoral visit which the minister has undertaken as his own faith project. He recently returned and telephoned me with a report. He recounted how he had taken quite a lot of time just to talk with and support our team leader in that particular country. Shortly after arrival, he realized that the leader and his wife, with their two young children, were under considerable stress. He talked with them about parenthood and the challenges of being both good parents and visionary leaders with significant responsibility. After spending several hours with them over a period of days, he offered some specific pastoral advice. Upon his return to the UK, he wanted to be sure that I knew about the situation and that I was aware of the advice he had offered.

In years past, I have known what it was, in circumstances similar to these, to be on the receiving end of criticism and accusation – 'Why don't you look after your people better?' Perhaps those accusations were coming from leaders who felt that they had been under attack. It wasn't uncommon for mission leaders regularly to criticize local church leaders for being too parochial, lacking in vision, not 'having God's heart for the world'. Thankfully, those accusations are not so common now, at least not from my perspective.

The growing respect between mission agencies and local churches, along with new coalition movements and networks of churches all provide a growing range of opportunities for partnership abroad. Partnership activities can include short-term mission teams, various construction and building projects, youth group excursions, pastoral visits extending right through the range to mature, long-range frontier missions projects.

We are convinced that every congregation ought to be able to identify clearly how they are making a contribution to completing the Great Commission. If they are unable to do so, then a change of heart might be required. Once the leadership and people are keen to be fully involved in missions, then prayer is in order. There are so many opportunities today, that it would be easy to jump into something that would not fit your particular local church. But God is more committed than we are to completing this task, so he will not fail to guide a willing group of people.

Our comments and illustrations in this chapter reveal that there are many issues to be considered when entering into partnership. But details will usually work out well if partners maintain a selfless love for one another. The structure and procedures go well where Christian love pervades the relationships.

PART THREE

TWELVE GOOD MEN AND TRUE

8

LEADERSHIP MAKES IT WORK

Evangelism strategies, networking opportunities, good relationships with the surrounding community – all these things are important in themselves, but churches will not grow and new churches will not be planted without good leadership. While democracy and equality are accepted as unassailable truths these days and might lead us to think that leadership is not very important, leadership is still essential for any group of people. That is especially true in churches. Without good leadership, a church cannot thrive.

The most important evidence to support the view that leadership is indispensable is the fact that Jesus focused his limited time and energies on the task of preparing leaders. The primary attention of his ministry was on the ones he picked to succeed him. Most of his recorded words were spoken to the apostles and he took them virtually everywhere he went. He also chose them with great care. Luke 6:12–16 records that Jesus spent a full night in prayer before choosing twelve followers whom he could train to lead the church. What was he looking for?

TWELVE MEN, GOOD AND TRUE

The fact that Jesus spent the entire night in prayer before making his choices is an indication that these were amongst

109

the most important decisions he would make. He was planning to prepare and launch a different order of leaders. They would be with him for less than three years, and then he would expect them to lead in the same manner as he was going to lead them. He had a short time to train them, then he would delegate to them the responsibility for the most precious of all the resources on this planet – the Church.

If we search the Bible and popular legend about the men Jesus chose, it seems that none of them had previously held any significant positions. Neither did they possess qualities that would have obviously distinguished them from their peers. So what was Jesus looking for?

Character

Surely the first thing Jesus was looking for was humility. So often, when he spoke to the religious leaders of the day, he made it clear that he came to those who knew they needed him. He had no time for those who thought they were already righteous and mature.

Once the twelve were chosen, Jesus embarked on a process of teaching, training, shaping and testing with the aim of producing godly character. He encouraged them, he rebuked them, he equipped them to deal with threatening situations, and throughout the three years, he shaped their characters. It is obvious that, at the outset, they did not have the maturity that Jesus would require of them. But they did have a desire to learn which set them apart from others.

When I first became a Christian, my older sister, who had been a Christian for some time, was of the opinion that I had a serious character defect. Being very keen to help me, she got hold of my Bible and underlined all of the passages that condemned pride. Her method of bringing the issue to my attention left something to be desired, but

110

she was right about the problem. Without a willingness to humble myself, I would have no potential for growth and maturity. Jesus wants followers who are humble and therefore teachable.

Though Jesus often spoke about humility, the disciples did not understand or apply his message. Towards the end of their three years together, Jesus and his disciples were walking from Galilee to Jerusalem, and Jesus was preparing them for the ordeal of the cross which lay ahead of them. Mark 10:32-34 records the words of Jesus as he explains that he is going to his death. But the power of pride and personal ambition is deafening. From verse 35, it is clear that the disciples weren't even listening to Jesus as he began to bare his heart and draw them into his passion. They were too busy disputing who would receive the positions of most honour in God's Kingdom.

In response to their distorted view of leadership, Jesus summarizes his teaching on leadership and describes the kind of person who will be great in his Kingdom. 'You know that those who are regarded as rulers of the Gentiles lord it over them, and their officials exercise authority over them. Not so with you. Instead, whoever wants to become great among you must be your servant, and whoever wants to be the first must be slave of all. For even the Son of Man did not come to be served, but to serve and, and to give his life as a ransom for many.'

There is evidence that even after this rebuke and then such clear teaching about servanthood, the disciples still didn't understand. Just a few days later, they were preparing to eat the Passover meal together, the Last Supper. Jesus knew that they had not yet understood this foundational message about leadership, so he arranged a dramatic illustration. We must not miss the significance of the fact that this teaching about servanthood was uppermost in his mind as they approached their last evening together. The occasion is recorded in John 13.

They must have been in the home of a wealthy sympathizer. It was large enough to have a room to accommodate them all, and the meal had been prepared and laid out by servants. There was just one task remaining before they reclined to eat: they must wash their feet. Washing in this manner was both a ritual and a practical necessity. No self-respecting Jew would eat without washing. And this was the most important meal of the year.

A servant had prepared the basin of water and a towel, but none of the servants were present to do the lowly task. The disciples must have waited somewhat awkwardly, as the record shows that the meal was ready, but they had not reclined at the table. Someone needed to wash their feet, but no one was willing to take up the task.

I suppose each of them had a good reason for not making a move. Perhaps Peter thought that, since John was the youngest, he should be the one to take up the basin and towel. John might have thought that it should be Thomas, or someone else – anyone but him because he was the closest to Jesus. But they all would have agreed on one thing: Jesus was the Teacher, the Leader, so it would be inappropriate for him to wash their feet.

It must have been an extremely awkward moment for each of them when Jesus removed his cloak and wrapped the towel around himself. Each must have wished desperately that he, or anyone but Jesus, had taken on the task. But in the silence of embarrassment they submitted to the service of Jesus. Until he came to Peter. As was often the case, Peter had the courage to say what the others were thinking. He expressed the embarrassment and humiliation of each one of them when he said, 'you shall never wash my feet.'

But Jesus pressed on with his service. When he had finished, he said, 'Do you understand what I have done for you? You call me "Teacher" and "Lord", and rightly so, for that is what I am. Now that I, your Lord and Teacher, have washed your feet, you should also wash one another's feet. I have set you an example, that you should do as I have done for you. I tell you the truth, no servant is greater than his master, not is a messenger greater than the one who sent him. Now that you know these things, you will be blessed if you do them.'

He said, 'Now that you know these things . . .' This phrase implies that the disciples had not previously understood this message of servant-hearted leadership. Jesus knew that, though he had taught the message many times before and though he had lived it before them for three years, they had not been able to see past their preconceived ideas about leadership. Finally, in the drama of this embarrassing demonstration, they had understood.

If this message was so difficult for the disciples to understand, will it be any easier for us? For this reason, we have chosen to labour this point. Servanthood leadership is difficult to understand. It runs contrary to the pride, position seeking and ambition of people who are gifted with leadership abilities.

Several years ago, I spent a few weeks with a church which was thriving. It had many positive qualities, but the thing that impressed me most was the leadership team. There were several highly gifted people who provided a remarkable balance for one another, and between them they possessed considerable breadth of ability. One of them had a ministry of teaching and another was a good administrator. Another one was often used by God in a healing ministry, while a fourth team member was a skilled pastoral counsellor.

The man who was the official minister was not necessarily the most capable or mature member of the team. But this didn't seem to be a problem as each member of the team made his or her contribution to the church. Some of the denominational leaders, however, did not like the model of leadership that was emerging. They took the minister aside and encouraged him more clearly to take the lead. Not long afterwards, he attended a conference where the teaching emphasized the superior role of the senior leader. The man who taught at the conference emphasized the need for each leader to teach a few others, while they served that leader in practical ways.

With this strong influence, the minister began to impose his will on the others. He required each of them formally to express their submission to him. Perhaps he sensed their reluctance, so he went even further. He began to require them to submit personal and business decisions to him. The predictable response to his invasive approach was the disintegration of the team. One by one, the exasperated members of the leadership team resigned and then left the church. Over this period of several months, he often preached against rebellion. He likened himself to Moses when Korah, Dathan and Abiram were resisting his leadership.

His continuous demands for recognition, submission and respect eventually emptied the pews and after a very painful season, he decided to resign. A thriving church had been reduced to less than 20 per cent of its original size and scores of people had been discouraged and hurt.

This kind of story has been acted out again and again because the problem of pride is so common. Jesus looked for humble men, but once they were chosen and appointed and began to see God's power at work through their lives, they became vulnerable to pride of position and a desire for recognition and honour.

When God calls a person to a leadership ministry, he calls that person to lay down his life for the sheep. In John 10, Jesus reveals the qualities of a good shepherd. It is a very demanding list of attitudes. That list is best summarized in verse 11, 'I am the good shepherd. The good shepherd gives his life for the sheep.' Though Jesus was referring to himself in a very literal manner, he was also setting a standard for all those who would follow him. The prime calling of leadership is service and sacrifice. Recognition and honour might occasionally accompany a calling to leadership, but they are never rights to be demanded.

In spite of the clear teaching of Jesus and the example of the apostles who followed him, we still tend to see leadership in terms of the benefits it brings to the leader – benefits of recognition, power and sometimes honour or even wealth.

A few years ago, we heard all about the sins and failures of certain American television evangelists. It is ironic that Christian leaders who were previously virtually unknown in the UK became household names once the press got wind of their failures. Two years before those failures a friend of mine, a very talented consultant called Richard, stood in the office of one of those evangelists. The evangelist was interested in employing Richard to help develop his organization. Over the years, Richard had devised several probing questions for initial interviews of this sort. Amongst them was, 'Who, in this organization, can say no to you and make it stick?' When he had heard the question, the evangelist gave a hearty laugh and called his personal assistant to come into the office. Then he instructed Richard to ask the question again and when the question was repeated, the two of then shared a good laugh. The evangelist became suddenly serious and leaned across the desk towards Richard and said, '*Nobody* says no to me!'

Richard's reply was straight to the point, 'Then I can be of no assistance to you.'

Leadership is not about honour, power and wealth. It is about humility and service. Jesus wants to form a strong and broad character in each of us. That character should include all of the fruits of the spirit: love, joy, peace, patience, kindness, goodness, faithfulness, gentleness and self-control. But the teachable heart that springs from humility is the foundational quality which leads on to all the other aspects of godliness.

Vision

Though we have emphasized the need for leaders to have godly character, that requirement is not unique to those called to leadership. Every Christian is subject to the commandment to be humble and holy. But the quality which marks out a leader from within any given group is vision. By vision we mean the ability to perceive and articulate a preferred future. In other words, an ability to imagine what the future of the group ought to look like and then be able to explain it to others in such a way that they can see it too.

The power of vision

Those two aspects alone do not provide a complete explanation of vision. There is more to it than seeing and explaining. A leader must also have faith that the future which he or she sees will come to pass, and then the leader must be able to infect the people with that faith. That infection of faith is the avenue through which the power of God is poured to actually bring the vision to pass.

The story of Moses and his leadership of the people of Israel is one of the most outstanding examples of vision.

Once God had finished preparing Moses, he came out of the desert with an inspirational vision. The vision he proclaimed was sufficient to stir a people who had been enslaved for more than three centuries. When he declared God's plans for their future, they believed that they could escape from their masters, trek across a desert, find a very desirable land, displace the inhabitants and possess that land. That is the power of vision.

It seems that Moses got his vision while he was all alone in a remote wilderness. Is that the usual way for God to give vision? No, that is an unusual way to shape a vision; and it didn't actually happen that way with Moses either. The vision he had was one that had been prophesied more than 400 years earlier. So what he declared to the families of Israel was a message they already understood. He simply stirred up the faith for them actually to believe that the prophecy could come to pass.

In the same way, any vision for a specific church or group of churches must be consistent with the Word of God. That Word has already made it clear that the Church is about growth and expansion. It is about reaching every person with the gospel and teaching them to obey everything that Jesus taught (Matt 28:18-20). This theme of growth is regularly presented as a primary characteristic of the Kingdom of God, of which the Church is a part. In the case of the parable of the sower (Mark 4), the growth is via multiplication of individuals. In the parable of the mustard seed (Matt 13) the Kingdom of God as a whole grows from insignificance to pre-eminence. In the parable of the yeast (Matt 13), the growth of the Kingdom is in the form of pervasive influence. In the parable which was given to King Nebuchadnezzar in a dream (Daniel 2), the growth of the Kingdom is presented as universal, in that it covers the whole earth. Within this general framework of growth, there is room for an almost infinite variety of ideas, plans and projects, but each one must make some contribution to the growth of the Church.

Energized by the Spirit

With the possibility of so many ideas, plans and projects, how can leaders know which of them is relevant to their own church? I used to visit regularly a church that was blessed with very gifted leadership. And yet the people had lost heart. Their demoralization was a mystery to me for some time, but after several visits, I realized that the people had been subjected to what I might call 'vision over-kill'. Their senior leader travelled often and widely and regularly ministered in churches which were large and growing. At most of these churches he identified some good vision which was at the heart of the growth. It might have been home Bible-study groups, or a community counselling ministry, or a dynamic youth ministry, or a particular approach to the Sunday morning meeting – the list could go on and on.

Almost every time the leader returned from a trip, he expressed great enthusiasm for some new vision for his home church. At first, this process produced encouragement and hope in the congregation and even some spurts of growth. But before one vision could be brought to a stage of maturity or completion, it was replaced by another. In the end, people listened to each new idea or plan of action with bemusement and at least a little cynicism. They didn't want any new vision until previous visions had been thoroughly pursued or recognized as a mistake.

How does the leader recognize which of the many possible visions are meant for his church? This fundamental question could be stated another way: 'What is God's vision for me and the people I lead or help to lead?'

Perhaps I can best shed some light on that question with a personal example. In 1989 I was one of the delegates from England to the Global Consultation On World Evangelization (GCOWE) in Singapore. It was a very good event throughout, but one optional afternoon session was especially important for me. Of the various possibilities, I decided to listen to Jim Montgomery, who was presenting a strategy called Disciple A Whole Nation (DAWN). Initially, I was interested but no more so than when I had previously attended other presentations on Christian broadcasting, denominational global plans and so on.

Within the first fifteen minutes of this session, my interest had turned to a deep excitement which in turn led to a personal commitment to adopt and adapt this strategy for England. As I listened to Jim's factual and unemotional presentation, I felt that God was speaking to me and saying, 'My church in England is ready for this strategy.'

I was in an environment that was full of different visions and plans, but I had not gone there to find one for me. I was already busy with previous visions. As Jim Montgomery spoke, though, his words struck me as though energized by the Spirit of God. From that time on I committed myself to initiate the DAWN strategy in England. Later I was very encouraged to find that at least one other English delegate in that session, Roger Forster, felt the same confirmation of God's Spirit within him. Together, we made a commitment to introduce this strategy as widely as possible within the Body of Christ in England. A few years later, we shared the joy of the first National DAWN Consultation where various churches, groups of churches and denominations committed themselves to plant at least 20,000 new churches before the end of the year 2000.

The DAWN vision was not something I dreamt up on my own. In fact, very few of us will ever initiate a thoroughly unique vision. Normally, we adopt and adapt a vision which we have seen or heard elsewhere. But of the many possible visions, a leader must learn to discover which one or ones are for him and the people he leads. The first factor in that discovery is what I have called the 'energizing of the Spirit', the moment when the Holy Spirit speaks to the leader and conveys that this is not just a good idea, it is God's idea for them.

God often uses a visionary environment to speak to a leader, just like he did with me at GCOWE in 1989. Because of that, every leader needs to have access to a visionary environment. That is one service which denominations or networks of churches should provide. But not every denomination or network of churches provides inspiration for vision and growth. However, there are many conferences, consultations and seminars which are widely available and can meet that need for leaders who do not have a regular environment of vision.

Making room for everyone

Good vision should aim to motivate and make a place for every person in the church. That is the point of it. If it enthuses the leader, but no one else, it will never succeed. This is where a small church has an advantage. It is easier for a small congregation to participate fully and it is easier than in a large congregation for the leader to be sure that everyone is working together.

Surely every Christian leader is aware of the 'body scriptures' in Rom 12, Eph 4 and 1 Cor 12-14. But they are also aware of the fact that 'every member doing his part' is much easier said than done. Good vision should enable each person to see where they fit and what contribution they can make to the future of the church. For that reason, it must be broad enough and the decision to adopt a particular vision must be processed well.

I was once closely involved with a fellowship that was led by a broad, visionary leader. He wasn't very good at managing all aspects of the vision, but he had attracted a good variety of people who were involved in many projects. They had an outreach bookstall, a coffee bar for youth, a tape ministry; others were involved in regular worship and outreach meetings in the town square and they ran a series of monthly interchurch worship and teaching meetings. Most of the people in the congregation had at least one project that gave them an opportunity to be active in some sort of outreach to others. It was a healthy church.

Eventually, the leader felt that he was called to move to another ministry and he began the process of turning the senior leadership over to another member of the leadership team. He was in the unusual position of having a number of capable leaders in the fellowship, so no difficulties were foreseen. Within a few months, however, nearly half of the congregation had left or were planning to leave in the immediate future. It was at that point that I happened to be visiting and, after my initial shock, began to ask questions.

Everyone seemed to respect the new leader, but I often heard the statement, 'He has no room in his plans for the ministry that God has laid on my heart.' The new leadership team had apparently spent time in prayer and planning and then announced a new beginning to the ministry of the church. All that could have been all right, but what they announced spelled the end for several good projects and activities, and left the people with nothing to do. When different people approached the leader, he said, 'I understand how you feel, but I have no heart for the kind of ministry you have been doing, and I don't see it fitting in the future of this church.' He was apparently a mature and able leader, but his vision was too narrow for the people and, in the end, he lost nearly half of his congregation. Good vision makes room for everyone.

The leader or leadership team must develop a good decision-making process before adopting a vision. There probably was a time when people were more responsive to directive leadership. A leader could stand up and say, 'This is what we are going to do,' and the people would do it. It rarely works that way these days. So the decision-making process is nearly as important as the appropriateness of the vision itself.

This process is quite a refined art, which is largely learned by experience with a particular group of people, but there are some general principles which can be outlined. The leader must take care about how he or she presents a new vision. It must be defined well enough for the people to be able to understand what it is all about, but it must not be fully defined or the people will feel that it is all 'signed, sealed and delivered'. When they feel excluded from the process of defining and adapting a vision, they will also feel less commitment to it.

If the people are going to have the maximum opportunity to 'buy into' the new vision, the leader will have to create a forum in which they can listen, ask questions, make suggestions and pray about the new proposals. There is at least a two fold reason for this need. Firstly they want to be assured that the leadership have really thought this through. They will also want to have time to understand the personal implications for themselves.

This process requires both discussion and group prayer. It may also require enough time between the first presentation and the final decision for people to think and pray about it individually.

The prayer and individual time are low-risk activities, but the open discussions can be high risk. When a leader presents a vision and then asks for questions and discussion, the few minutes that follow can mean life or death to the vision. The possibilities of life for the vision increase dramatically if the leader has really thought through the implications of the vision. It also helps a lot if he or she presents it in such a way that people see a willingness to make changes and adaptations when necessary. But the most important assurance for the life of the vision at this point must come from the confidence that this is not just a good idea, it is something that has come from God.

Whether it is lack of leadership vision or the difficulties of introducing a vision to the congregation, a recent study of local church attitudes to mission found that 63 per cent had no form of vision statement whatsoever. It may be that the declining church in Europe is an embodiment of the often quoted proverb, 'Without vision, the people perish.'

For Christian leaders, character and vision are the most important prerequisites. As Christian leaders undergo what we might call spiritual formation on the inside, their activity, ministry and responsibility will start to define a role for them in the Church at large. In the next chapter we shall look at the various roles and functions of Christian leadership.

9

THE FUNCTION AND ROLE OF LEADERSHIP

It has always been the joke in my family that our wealth of knowledge was gleaned primarily from old copies of the *Readers Digest*. I remember in one old copy one of those true life stories, which furnishes me with an apt introduction to this chapter on the role and function of leadership.

A vicar was moving on to a new parish, and on the Sunday before he was due to depart an elderly parishioner approached him after the service, clutched his hand warmly and told him how sorely she would miss him as the new incumbent wouldn't be nearly as good. In line with the true leadership characteristics of humility outlined in the last chapter, he replied that he was sure that that wouldn't be the case. When the old lady insisted it would be, he asked her how she knew, to which she replied 'I've had seven vicars at this church and none of them has been as good as the one before.'

I can remember experiencing exactly the same phenomenon at my Church of England primary school. The retiring vicar was a much loved white-haired grandfather with countless anecdotes drawn from years of ministry and travel. His successor was a young man who quite spectacularly failed to build a rapport with us juniors. Today he is a bishop. Which of the two was the more successful? I wouldn't like to be seen to judge in this particular instance: depending on your perspective, it could be either.

It was back in the 1950s that Dr Donald McGavran first drew attention to the fuzzy criteria by which missionaries were assessed. He discovered that the average missions report contained far more about the progress of the missionary and his family in learning a new language and coping with a new culture than it did about the extension of the gospel and the building of the church. Dr McGavran caused all sorts of controversy at the time by applying management skills to the mission field. However, the Church Growth Movement which he started has led to a far greater effectiveness in those missions societies which have applied his principles. Church Growth thinking has also defined certain criteria by which the local church can gauge its success in terms of growth, although its critics will still say that there are qualitative aspects of local church life that can't be measured with a slide rule.

In a sense this is true. There is certainly a depth to the gospel that the Church is here to incarnate, and it is far less easy to quantify this than the oft-counted 'bottoms on pews'. Even so, there must be criteria by which we can assess the relative merits of different approaches to leadership. The first step towards such a criteria is a clear biblical understanding of the objectives of various roles and functions of leadership. Once we know the goal of a particular leadership role, an individual can start to assess his or her suitability for the particular job. After all, there is no reason why a good bishop need have been a good vicar or why a good vicar should be promoted to bishop.

OFFICE, POSITION AND AUTHORITY

We have already stated the authors' assertion that a congregation of believers can be a church regardless of any particular ecclesiological structures. Most church structures are expressed in terms of leadership office, position and authority. However, while we do not believe that a church needs a particular leadership structure to be a church, we do believe that certain types of leadership are essential for the church to fulfil its purpose on earth.

It is abundantly clear from scripture that church leadership is more to do with maturity, responsibility and service than with position and kudos. Interestingly the words 'leader' or 'leadership' does not occur in the New Testament (unless you use the New International Version, where 'leadership' is used twice to translate *episkope*, more accurately translated as 'overseership'). All the words used to describe various church leadership roles fall into one of two categories: those that relate to responsibility and stewardship for the church or congregation, and those that relate to service. In the former category are *episkopos*, normally translated 'bishop' or 'overseer' and *presbuteros*, normally translated 'elder'. In the latter category are *diakonos* and *huperetes*, which are translated in various ways such as 'servant', 'minister' and 'deacon'. Paul then lists five types of leadership ministries which represent the full range of service to the church: apostle, prophet, evangelist, teacher and pastor. We shall think further on what these ministries are and their relevance to the local congregation later in this chapter.

This is an important division of leadership function. There are those whose primary role is to carry the responsibility for a particular part of the Church, and those whose primary role is to minister. These two spheres of leadership are not mutually exclusive, but neither should we assume that they are coincident. In practice, we would hope to see a sensible balance of these two distinct functions of church leadership in every Christian leader, so that the local 'elders' are also ministers and that gifted teachers or evangelists are accountable to a particular part of the church, be it local or wider.

In scripture, individuals are given different leadership titles in different situations. Barnabas is a pastor, a teacher, an evangelist, a prophet and an apostle. Peter and John write as elders of the church, but are also apostles. In Acts 20, Paul calls together the 'elders' and then refers to them as 'over-seers' or 'bishops' (it is interesting that there have been all sorts of schism over whether churches should have elders rather than bishops and vice versa). The interchangeability of these titles for various Christian leaders indicates that we cannot see these offices as cut and dried.

The fact that the first Christian leaders needed to operate in different leadership roles according to context, probably goes against some of our subconscious ideas of ministry. We tend to think that someone with a ministry gift ought to be allowed to get on with using it. This may often be true, but in Eph 4, it explicitly states that these ministries are gifts for building up the body of Christ, not for keeping an indi-vidual on the spiritual gravy train for the course of their natural life. So if a local leader is by nature a pastor, he needs to ask the question, 'Does this church need more pastoring at the moment, or does it have a greater need?' He or she may need to do the work of an evangelist for a while, or let an evangelist loose on the church. Seen in these terms, teachers are not teachers because they can write great books (like this one!) or give erudite lectures. They are teachers if they serve the body of Christ and build it up in the knowl-edge and understanding of Jesus. Evangelists are not even evangelists because they run missions and lead people to Jesus. They are evangelists if their service to the Church enables it to evangelize.

When assessing the role of an individual Christian leader,

the distinction between responsibility and ministry can be useful. Leaders can start to focus the fuzziness of their own objectives by deciding whether their primary vocation at any particular moment is responsibility for a local church or ministry in the Church. The confusion of these two functions gives rise to the common assumption that a pastor should lead a local church or that a local church leader is the pastor or teacher. Once we have an idea of how our leadership time and energy should be split between these two functions, we need to have some idea of what constitutes success in them.

ELDERS AND BISHOPS

The ideas of Church responsibility are expressed biblically by the words 'elder, 'bishop' or 'overseer'. Today denominations might use other titles to convey this responsibility, such as 'vicar' or even 'minister' or 'pastor', or the biblical words with a particular historical or theological understanding. The title is unimportant, and for the sake of clarity, we shall use the word 'elder' to refer to Christian leaders who carry the responsibility for a part of the church.

It is the job of the elder, recognized by virtue of their maturity or affirmation by other leaders, to be the custodian of the congregation's well-being and development. The responsibility aspect of church leadership is well summed up in Heb 13:17, where the congregation is urged to submit to those who watch over their souls, who must give an account for the health of the congregation. It is the eldership of a congregation who are responsible for its short- and long-term vision, though they may need some help from the prophets to define it. Interestingly, in a recent survey of 400 Protestant churches in the United Kingdom, it was found that over 60 per cent had no form of vision statement. As custodians of the vision, it is not the elders' job to do all the work and ministry, but rather to make sure that the congregation gets all the service it needs to fulfil that vision.

Springfields Church was planted under the 'oversight' of curate Tim Humphrey from Holy Trinity Parish Church in Wallington in Surrey. Within two years it had outgrown its building and had 200 regular members, putting it in the largest 10 per cent of Anglican churches. In an interview for the *DAWN News Bulletin*, the magazine for the DAWN Strategy in England, Tim explained that one of the keys to their success was the drawing of others into ministry.

He explains 'Being a Church of England clergyman, it does not always come easily to release others into areas of ministry and take on the role of trainer and equipper, rather than "doer". As the church has grown, the need for small group leaders, capable of taking some pastoral responsibility, has been paramount. Right now, training is probably one of my highest priorities.'

He goes on, 'Because I see my gifts mainly as a pastor and teacher, I have noticed with horror how easily evangelism falls off the bottom of the urgent list! A significant development for us therefore has been a *sustainable* "friendship evangelism" strategy.'

Tim had instinctively understood that his responsibility for the embryonic congregation was to make sure that it received and expressed the ministries that it needed to grow, rather than try to provide those ministries himself. Despite being a pastor, he needed to see others released into pastoral ministry to cope with growth. Despite not being an evangelist, he ensured that an evangelism programme was being developed and pursued within the church.

The idea that it is not the local leader's job to be, do and provide everything that the congregation requires to grow into 'the fullness of the stature of Christ' is an important conclusion. As we explore the necessity for, and function of, the service ministries, it is important that the person with leadership responsibility for the local church does not feel compelled to be pastor, teacher, evangelist, prophet and apostle, though they should make sure that their congregation receives input from these ministries and that the congregation exercises them (albeit embryonically) within itself.

Barry, who would see himself in the classic pastor-teacher mould, informed me that a colleague had told him years before that the primary responsibility of the local church leader was to lead the church. Pastoring and teaching came second. Barry now leads a large church and has a number of significant ministries operating within its leadership team. This church has been instrumental in leading other congregations in a town-wide evangelism and church-planting strategy, and it is getting directly involved in overseas missions, to the extent that it is trying to incorporate as a missionary society.

Barry's colleague went on to become General Secretary of the Baptist Union. If Barry had decided that he should just be a pastor-teacher for his local congregation, it may never have grown. But by drawing other ministries into the church from outside, both permanently and temporarily, and by entrusting ministry responsibility to younger Christians, Barry has seen his church go from strength to strength.

Being an elder is less about gifts and abilities and more about discipline, commitment and maturity. The founding elder of one large church prayed every day for every member of his church by name until it reached eighty people. Ministry is more about gifts and abilities but does not require the same depth of commitment to a group of people as eldership. Recognizing this should help free elders from the feeling that they must be ministerial super-stars. They can let congregation members exercise their fledgling or mature gifts in leadership before they attain the responsibility and maturity of an elder. This also means that an elder can draw on the wider body of Christ for ministe-rial input, even though those that provide the input won't share the same commitment to the local congregation.

This book will appeal mainly to those who have some sort of local leadership responsibility to provide the ministry needs of their congregation. We believe that the fivefold ministries expounded in Eph 4 are the key for helping both small and large congregations fulfil their vital role in the big vision. We don't need people going around with these five titles, but we do need the activity and anointings which are represented by these ministries at work in our churches. We need to examine the necessity and role of the fivefold ministries so those with eldership responsibility can make sure that their church is receiving from them.

THE FIVEFOLD MINISTRIES

There is something about the fivefold ministries that is vital to the church fulfilling the Great Commission and there-fore, ultimately, its destiny. If the Church is going to grow into 'the fullness of Christ', then we need the ministries that Paul explicitly states are for this. Not every ministry need be found in every local church, and this was as true in the New Testament as it is today. But local elders need to make sure that their churches are being regularly exposed to these ministries and that they make room for them in the life of their churches.

In simple terms, pastors are needed by the Church to lead her into love and unity, which are fundamental to the world knowing who we are and believing our message (John 13:35, 17:21). Teachers are needed to lead her into know-ledge and truth so that one day 'the earth shall be filled with the knowledge of the glory of God as the waters cover the sea'. Evangelists are needed to lead the Church into growth. Prophets are needed to lead the Church into the future. Apostles are needed to lead the Church into multiplication. In more recent centuries, the title 'missionary' had been equated in some circles with the New Testament function of 'apostle'. Whether this is appropriate or not, the association of the two functions gives us an indication of the relevance of the apostolic ministry to the missionary congregation.

AN ECUMENICAL ISSUE

The biggest problem with our assertion that the fivefold ministries need to be restored if the church is to be success-ful in its mission, is the very divisive nature of this statement when unity is also important. Just a few years ago the World Council of Churches asserted that the threefold ministries, of bishop, priest and deacon, have the basis of the historic church's unity. If everybody accepted bishops, priests and deacons then we could all be one happy people. The sepa-ratists should give up their ideas of presbyteries or whatever they thought Church order should be and fit in. Those who would not do this did not find it too helpful to be put into the position where they were being accused of being divisive.

Why do we need apostles, prophets, evangelists, pastors and teachers? Can't we make do with bishops, priests and deacons?

The unity of the church is fundamental to its ultimate success in mission, but the structure of the church is not the basis of its unity. Our common revelation of Jesus as Christ and the indwelling presence of his Holy Spirit are the basis of our unity. The kinds of ministries that rise up within the Spirit's unity are not necessarily the glue that holds the church together. Besides, 'bishops' and 'deacons' are simply ways of expressing the leadership functions of responsibility and of service, and in that sense are not even structurally incompatible with our assertion that within the ranks of servant leadership we need pastors, teachers, evangelists, prophets and apostles. The addition of 'priest' to this structure implies an element of mediation in church leadership. Whilst there is truth in this idea (a responsible leader ought to be pushing further into the presence of God on behalf of his or her congregation), we should not make a separate issue of it. It is the job of the whole church to be the vicarious Body of Christ to the world, a leaders' priestly function is more a matter of degree than a special function.

Even in nonconformist circles, the idea of modern-day apostles is still contentious, despite being around for over a century. At the beginning of the twentieth century, the issue caused a division in the Pentecostal Movement between the Apostolic Denomination and the rest, who repudiated the need for restoration of the fivefold ministries. Today many Pentecostals ignore the adamant theology laid down by their founding fathers and accept apostolic ministry.

The Latter Rain ministries of the 1940s and 1950s also emphasized the necessity of apostles as well as prophets, evangelists, pastors and teachers in church leadership. Of course in certain quarters of the church, Latter Rain is synonymous with heresy and the issue of the fivefold ministries can therefore be ignored as wrong by association.

With the rise of the charismatic movement during the 1970s, there was a conscious division between restoration churches, which set up new congregations and looked for the restoration of these ministries, and charismatic churches which remained in the historic denominations, and felt it was unnecessary to make a big issue as to whether they were restored or not.

With all this controversy it might seem prudent to ignore this issue, but unfortunately it is important. It is not merely an academic subject whereby way-out theologians argue for present-day apostles, and traditional theologians argue against them. If God's Word indicates, as it seems to, that we need apostles for the Church to complete the Great Commission by attaining her full stature, then we need to examine the issue carefully.

Of course we also need unity. 'I pray that they may be one . . . that the world might believe' is an essential element for world evangelization, and we should not treat unity cheaply or contentiously. When Jesus prayed for unity he got it within six hours. In the crucifixion, all divisions are gone and there is no excuse for separatism, but equally there is no place to say that the threefold ministry is more important than the fivefold ministries or any other ministry, or that ditching one in favour of another would at last create unity. Unity is a gift to be preserved, not created. Unity is key to success in mission, but it is complementary not contradictory to our need for the fivefold ministries in our churches.

THE EXEGETICAL BASIS

Accepting that our assertion need not and should not be divisive, what is its biblical basis? Despite statements made in some commentaries, there is an exegetical basis for the

THE FUNCTION AND ROLE OF LEADERSHIP

continuing role of the fivefold ministries right through the church age. To make this point forcefully, we need to remind ourselves of what Ephesians actually says about the operation and purpose of these ministries.

> When he ascended on high, he led captive a host of captives, and he gave gifts to men . . . And he gave some as apostles, some as prophets and some as evangelists and some as pastors and teachers, for the equipping of the saints for work of service to the building up of the body of Christ until we attain to the unity of the faith and of the knowledge of the Son of God, to a mature man to the measure of the stature which belongs to the fullness of Christ. Eph 4:8–13.

The exegetical necessity for these ministries is that Jesus gave them *after* his ascension. There were 'apostles of the incarnation' (Luke 6:13): these were the twelve who laid the foundation of doctrine on which we stand in the New Testament and they can never be replaced. There were 'apostles of the resurrection' (1 Cor 15), who were sent forth to declare as eyewitnesses that Jesus had risen from the dead. It would even seem that there were 'pre-incarnation apostles' sent before Jesus, which he refers to in Luke 11:49. However, the apostles of Eph 4 are 'apostles of the ascension'. If Jesus gave the fivefold ministries as gifts to the Church from heaven, *after* his ascension then there is no reason whatsoever why the ministry of apostles should not continue right the way through the church age.

The passage from Ephesians is quite specific that these ministries are all given until 'we all' attain the unity, knowledge and maturity of the fullness of Christ. If we have not yet reached the fullness of the stature of Christ then we need these ministries, including apostles, for God's purpose for the Church to be fulfilled. This result can hardly be gainsaid: apostles were and are gifts to the Church, given from the ascension with a role to play in the building up of the Church until Jesus comes again. We understand that, in some church circles, the term 'apostle' is not likely to be accepted as a description of a current ministry in the near future. We do not wish to demand that the *term* be used, as long as the ministry is being exercised freely.

THE ESCHATOLOGICAL PURPOSE

We have already seen that the big vision of the world mission is tied up with God's plan to reconcile all things in Jesus. The context of Eph 4 is precisely this plan. It is the destiny and purpose of the Church to come up to Christ's fullness. Fullness in breadth as we spread into every tribe, tongue, kindred, people and nation; fullness in depth as we get deeper and deeper into the knowledge of God through Jesus Christ, deeper in God and deeper into the world until the Church reaches its full stature.

The fivefold ministries are explicitly given to the Church for the fulfilment of this purpose. The eschatological purpose of apostles makes them essential, along with the prophets, evangelists, pastors and teachers, if Christ is going to be manifest in all his fullness throughout the earth and down all our streets. If any of these ministries is missing from our local church then it is vital that the elders find ways of introducing their input. The authors can not pretend to be able to give a complete description of the activity and anointing of these ministries, but we offer the following descriptions to help identify them in our churches.

PASTORS AND TEACHERS

Of all the various leadership ministries, those of pastor and teacher probably need the least comment. They have long been recognized by all denominations and churchmanships as relevant modern local church ministries. Part of the reason that they are such universally accepted positions is because they have been seen as predominantly concerned with the internal spiritual life of the church in a context that has not for many centuries acknowledged a need for growth, change or multiplication, the domain of the other Ephesian ministries. However, the idea that pastors and teachers are solely concerned with the inner life of the congregation does not stand up to biblical scrutiny, and very few Bible colleges would impart such an idea to their trainees. Nevertheless, the view is often reinforced in the minds of the congregation by the subsequent non-participation of their graduate pastor-teacher in evangelism. Good pastors and good teachers find ways of pastoring and teaching those who are not yet saved.

In Ephesians, Paul entreats the Church to walk in a manner worthy of her calling, (Eph 4:1-3). The character of the ideal church in Paul's description is one of love and forbearance, gentleness and humility. For that character to grow to its full stature, pastors are required. The pastor helps the Church become more forbearing, more loving, more able to walk in humility and more able to be gentle. Many churches do not demonstrate much love, forbearance, gentleness, humility or patience, and these are usually churches which are badly pastored. If the people we call pastors are not discipling us to love one another, then they are not the pastors given by the ascended Jesus to his church. Good pastoring preserves 'the unity of the spirit and the bond of peace.' Pastors help in the reconciling of all things in Christ; they are here to help people to be one.

But it is not just those in the church that pastors are supposed to help to become one. As the Good Shepherd, Jesus' pastoral heart wept for the whole of his city. Following on from this example, good pastors develop links with their local communities as an expression of the fact that real love does not just love its own (Matt 5:46). One of the first graduates of the four-year ministry degree in church planting run by Spurgeons College recently found himself planting a church on the Isle of Dogs at the height of the racial tension that led to the election of the first British National Party local councillor in the country. He soon found that those stirring up trouble were deliberately using religion as a racially divisive tool. He felt that positive action was needed, so the churches in the area found ways of making contact with Muslim and Hindu leaders and co-ordinating the plaiting of hundreds of ribbons into little rainbow pendants which became a symbol of racial harmony. The BNP later lost its seat and actually blamed the activity of the church among non-Christian working class whites for its loss. In this way, Steve and other pastors on the Isle of Dogs were helping a largely non-Christian community grow in love.

Pastoring the wider community is an important part of incarnating the good news. As a Nonconformist who has had the pleasure of working with many Anglican priests, I have observed that it is still true that the Anglican 'dog collar' opens up avenues for pastoral contact that other ministerial regalia cannot reach. Pastors whose spiritual heritage is second- or third-generation secessionist will have to work harder at this aspect of pastoral ministry.

Having outlined the loving character of the Church, Eph 4 goes on:

There is one body, one Spirit, just as you were called one hope of your calling, one Lord, one faith, one baptism, one God and Father of all who is over all, through all and in all and to each of us is given grace according to the measure of the Christ's gift. Eph 4:4-7

We also need teachers because the Church is not only a loving Church, it is a creedal Church. There are specific things that we believe, one body, one Spirit, one Lord, one faith, etc. The Church of Jesus Christ knows that it is meant to believe something specific and not just anything. While we may misunderstand bits of Leviticus, there are fundamentals on which we all agree, including the conviction that there is truth to be discovered. Teachers help us grow in our knowledge of God and keep the Church anchored to the revelation of God in Jesus.

Like the pastor, the teacher must not fall into the trap of assuming that his or her gifts should be reserved for the benefit of the Church. Jesus taught literally tens of thousands of people, but only a few hundred could be considered his disciples.

A few years back, I found myself on a youth-work team with two card-carrying evangelists. Under my friend Paul's leadership, we spent most of our time doing evangelism; my role was regularly educating and teaching our audience (whether captive in a schoolroom or free to wander off). On this foundation, one of my friends could preach for a response. Interestingly, I have used many of the lessons prepared for those non-Christians just as effectively with Christians. Good teachers make truth accessible to all, they don't confuse half the congregation with their evident scholarship. While at university, I remember wondering how Jesus taught the masses without easy reference to a pocket

Septuagint during one rather dry yet biblically thorough Christian Union meeting. A good knowledge of the scriptures is one of the tools of a good teacher, but Jesus would not have made a good carpenter if he spent all day polishing his hammer, and so we should not equate biblical scholarship with the ministry of teaching.

EVANGELISTS

The evangelist has a ministry that is receiving increasing recognition in Europe's historic denominations as a valid local church ministry that has been too long neglected. We have seen the necessity of pastors and teachers for the growth of the Church in love and knowledge. But primarily the Body of Christ grows through evangelism. The work of the Church is not to love one another – that is a grace. The work of the Church is to make disciples of all nations. That work is done by the help of evangelists, and a church that loses its evangelists stops working. It may enjoy the benefits of community, but it will lose its sense of purpose if it doesn't keep pushing out to see the boundaries of the Church extended until the whole world is covered with the good news of Jesus. Many churches have stopped working because they haven't got an evangelist.

After a hard day at work, you have every good reason to do nothing at all in the evening, but an evangelist banging on your door may coerce you begrudgingly out to share your faith. You don't like being dragged out, but afterwards you are thrilled to have shared in the work of God. You are glad to be in the business of evangelism and that there is an evangelist keeping you going. The church needs evangelists.

In 1994 the Evangelical Alliance in the United Kingdom

commissioned a report into the place of evangelism and mission in the local church. The results were fascinating. While 70 per cent of church leaders agreed that sharing the good news with their immediate neighbourhood was their church's primary function, only 25 per cent of churches had leaders whose main role was to encourage local evangelism. While 85 per cent of leaders indicated that their members were regularly encouraged to share their faith, only 38 per cent of churches had any form of ongoing personal evangelism training.

This discrepancy between ideal and practice could be illustrated again and again from the findings of the research. The research also showed that there was a perceived increase in missions orientation as opposed to maintenance orientation over the last five years. It seems that missions work is getting onto the agendas of more and more churches, but that the ministry mix of their leaderships teams is still too pastorally orientated. In the survey, 77 per cent of leaders indicated that they always gave as much time to their congregations' problems as was wanted of them.

Just as we must not make the mistake of assuming that a pastor or teacher's ministry is all internal, it is important that churches do not assume that the evangelist's role is purely for the outsider. I was once present in a church when it formally recognized one of its members as their evangelist. The pastor asked him to stand and a few of the elders prayed for him. After this, he found himself in a curious situation where the church felt good about itself because it was one of the few in the town with a recognized evangelist, but where he himself had no access or place in the leadership decisions of the church. The last I heard of him he was attending a different church. His story could be repeated many times over. Sometimes it is the fault of the evangelist who is so concerned with the goats that he deliberately distances himself from the rest of the flock so as not to smell too much of sheep. Other times it is the fault of the pastor who has not realized that the evangelist is equally a gift given to build up the church.

It is my experience that congregations that are continually exposed to the preaching of evangelists have a ar greater sense of excitement about their faith which flows from the continual reminder of the grace of God seen in the cross and its application to all parts of their life. This is not surprising; evangelists only really have the one message, it just so happens it's the most exciting and important one.

PROPHETS

The role of the prophet has been recognized by a good number of denominations for well over a century. The role was also relevant in the early church well into the second century as an itinerant ministry. However, as with apostles, it seems that the respect and authority coupled with the lack of accountability that went with this itinerancy led to widespread abuse of the position and subsequent suspicion of the title on the part of local church elders. In many ways, the function has survived in the Roman Catholic mystical tradition and the Protestant preacher, though neither really does full credit to the role.

The Church has not yet achieved its destiny. Its end is to contain the fullness of Christ, to reach the knowledge of the Son of God in depth. There is a process at work: the Church is not just a static worship club or a bunch of people who have found a little bit of help to get through the veil of tears into which they were pitched without being asked. Neither is it a philosophical debating society winning a few arguments and gaining a few converts. The Church is in business to go places.

To the first century Jew, *ekklesia* carried ideas of the Old Testament congregation of Israel on its way to nationhood. Without Moses, that church forgot where they were going and who they were. Local churches need prophets to keep them moving forward and remind them of what they are supposed to be. The purposes of the human race are vested in the Church attaining the full stature of Christ. We need prophets to get there, to point out the areas in which we do not match up to this stature, to steer and guide our congregations, to show us where we are on the journey and lead us into unknown territory.

From what we know of the role of prophets in the early church, it would seem that they operated primarily in an itinerant manner. This is not surprising. Unlike the teacher who can work through a programme of material, the prophet may get stuck with one message for some time. We also know that prophets had a particular role in worship, being given freedom to break regular patterns and prayers. Today, many would acknowledge a prophetic anointing on certain worship and prayer leaders. Finally, it is also clear that they were expected to bring a revelational utterance on which the congregation would act as long as it was consistent with scripture.

To summarize the characteristics of prophetic ministry, prophets are those who have a strong emphasis on what we should be, compared with what we are; whose teaching is inspirational and requires a response; whose ministry pushes the Church forward in prayer and worship; and who have a well-developed revelational gift.

APOSTLES

Like the prophets, the function of apostle was recognized at least into the second century, when all who could have seen Jesus in the flesh were long dead. In the *Didache*, a second-century document purporting to contain the codified teaching of the Twelve on issues of church order, we read instructions on how to receive apostles and prophets. By this time there seems to be considerable cynicism about their motives, and the *Didache* gives all sorts of criteria by which one can tell if an apostle is false or genuine, and it doesn't allow them to stay too long in one church. The roots of this suspicion and misuse of the function can be found in Rev 2, where John warns about false apostles, but makes the assumption that there are still other valid apostles around even though he is the only one of the Twelve left alive. The important point is simply that, way past the death of the original Twelve, the early church still recognized the function of apostleship and did not write the obituary to the office of apostle with the death of John.

If we need pastors to lead congregations into love, teachers to lead them into truth, evangelists to lead them into growth and prophets to lead them into the future, then what is the role of the apostle? The apostle leads us into multiplication. Biblically, it seems that the apostles given after the ascension have at least four important characteristics.

First, they are 'sent'. Apostle actually means 'someone sent forth'. As gifts to the Church, they carry within themselves the mandate to go; separate them from the local church and the local church forgets the urgency of that mandate.

Second, apostles seem to be people who carry a balance of the other four ministries in their own. Paul starts his ministry as a teacher and prophet leading the church in

Antioch, eventually he is sent forth as an apostle and we see him as evangelist and pastor. Similarly, we can trace a development in Barnabas, from encouraging congregation member through pastor, teacher, evangelist and prophet until he is finally called an apostle (Acts 4:36, 9:22-30, 13:1, 13:46-49, 14:14).

Third, it seems that they have the ability to release the ministry gifts in others. So we find Paul nurturing a series of travelling companions who, church history and the Bible tell us, follow his example.

Fourth, they have the authority to appoint elders, at least in the churches that they have planted. It is easy to see how this aspect of apostolic leadership has been absorbed into certain denominational institutions. This is not surprising, as apostleship seems to be a ministry which operates translocally, and denominations are structures designed to enable the Church to function this way as well. Because apostles sum up the other ministries they are able to reproduce them all in the churches in which they operate. This is of course why we so often associate apostles with pioneering situations, and some sections of the church have equated early church apostles with modern missionaries.

If an apostle oversees the establishing of new congregations, the development of a balance of all the leadership ministries will be ensured. Apart from the grace of God, if a pastor plants a church, he or she will pastor and pastor the flock to death; if an evangelist plants a church, he or she will wear it out with work; if a prophet plants a church, he or she will blow it up with a few broadsides; and if a teacher plants a church, he or she will lecture everybody to sleep with their superior erudition and knowledge. But if an apostle plants a church, his or her balance of prophet, evangelist, pastor and teacher will build the sort of church that will nurture and produce other churches and that will produce all sorts of ministries. After planting the church in Ephesus, Paul leaves them and commends them to carry on the work that he had modelled for them. By the time Revelation was written, there were six new churches in the surrounding towns. Paul's apostolic ministry had made them a missionary church equipped with the leaders required for multiplication.

Apostolic ministry is not just about pioneering. As an 'apostle to the Gentiles', Paul's ministry in local congregations kept their attention on those that were beyond the current reach of the Church, won concessions for the Gentile way of doing things and built bridges between congregations in different places. Apostles are not just missionaries, they are leaders whose ministry builds missionary congregations. Missionary congregations are always looking at ways of reaching new people groups and communities, whether different strata of society, un-churched housing estate, new cities or new nations.

In a recent study of Baptist church plants in the UK, it was discovered that the initiative to plant onto a new housing estate or into a new area had normally come from within the congregation rather than from the leader. The reverse was true when a new church was planted because the mother church had become overcrowded – in these cases, the leaders were more likely to have taken the initiative than the church members. World-wide, the DAWN strategy has shown that church planting is a crucial element in the evangelization of an area. Reproduction is as much a sign of spiritual maturity as it is of physical maturity. Not all adults will have children, but they all have that potential. Likewise a mature church must have the potential of extending beyond its current context by the multiplication of cells and congregations, and this is encouraged by apostolic input. Both our congregations and their leaders need to be open to this input. A church that receives apostolic input is looking not only for its ministry to grow in size, but in variety.

The emergence of a number of aggressively church-planting, new denominations in the United Kingdom and the United States since the 1960s has led many to credit the founding leaders of these new streams with apostolic ministry. However, it is not always necessary to leave a denomination and join a New Church to receive apostolic ministry. Many churches from historic denominations take advantage of New Church training programmes and leadership conferences. In addition, we are beginning to see the emergence of similar ministries within most Protestant denominations. While the ministry of apostle is not common, the church-planting movement is bringing the attention of the church at large to those who have this ministry, and large interchurch events are giving an increasing number of congregations access to it.

Because apostleship seems to be made up of a balance of all four of the other ministries described by Paul in Ephesians, it is not unreasonable to assume that it will never be as common as the other four. For that reason a local congregation needs to look to the wider church to receive this ministry, rather than looking to put an apostle onto the payroll.

THE LEADERSHIP TEAM

Finally, a few words about the shape, size and responsibility of a local church leadership team. Every congregation needs an overseer or two — while ministers come and go, these are the people who have a long-term commitment to this particular part of the Church. Normally, these elders will have been recognized by the wider church, perhaps by the laying on of hands of other leaders or by the local congregation itself. It is the responsibility of this eldership to build a ministry team to serve the church.

In this chapter, we have asserted that the restoration of the fivefold ministries hold the key to releasing both the local church and the Universal Church into effective missions. It is not necessary however, for the leadership team in every local church to be made up of five people who carry these titles. In many ways apostles, prophets, pastors, teachers and evangelists are like footballers in a good team: they all use the same basic set of skills and techniques, but different positions use those skills in different ways to perform different tasks. Likewise with Christian ministry, leaders should have the basic skills to play in any position, but they will by nature and training fall more easily into some roles than others. A leadership team should try to balance enough maturity, skill and ability to play each of these roles to a level and ability appropriate to the local church.

In a small church it is unlikely that this team will contain a full complement of the ministries described in Ephesians. This is not a failure, it seems to be the biblical and historical norm. We have already noted that the *Didache* treats apostles and prophets as itinerant rather than local ministries, although biblically there is precedent for an apostle or prophet to be part of the leadership of a larger church, such as Antioch, Ephesus or Jerusalem.

For the small church, the most commonly needed addition to the leadership structure is the evangelist. If the research on attitudes towards mission in the local church as cited earlier, holds true for most congregations, then three out of every four local churches do not have an evangelist on their leadership team. I was told by one pastor that the problem was that evangelist was such a rare calling, but in my experience this is not true. There are literally hundreds of evangelists working out their ministry in specialist agencies because they have so few models of local church evangelistic leadership. Many of the agencies for which these evangelists work are looking for ways of linking with local churches, and they might well be open to seconding leaders with a view to their joining a church permanently or to helping develop emerging evangelistic gifts within a congregation.

Even though a church may not be big enough to have an apostle or a prophet on its leadership team, it can aid the input of these ministries by the inclusion of those with prayer, worship or missions responsibility in the leadership decision-making process, and by giving these people some freedom to organize special events for the congregation. If finances allow, it is often worthwhile sending those with this type of pragmatic leadership on conferences with those who have a proper anointing for it. In this way, the congregation may suddenly find that they have a prophetic worship leader instead of just a pianist!

A local church leadership team needs to see itself as a temporary coalescing of relationships which extend into the congregation and out into the wider church. The team members need not all hold equal responsibility and authority. Some will minister on the team for a season and move on, others will maintain a continuity of vision over a longer period of time. The team should not be a static little club for the stalwart members of the congregation, maintaining an exclusive right to cure souls in their 'small corner'. It should be a flexible group, continually looking for growth and development of its gifts and maturity through openness to each other and to leaders in the wider church. The team acts as the lens of a camera, focusing the ministries of the wider church into the congregation, leaving the image of Jesus it has seen imprinted on its members. It also acts as an incentive to aspiring leaders by being open to them to take on various levels of responsibility.

In a small church with a big vision there will be a continual turn-around of the leadership team. As team members go off on the mission field, plant churches or just come to the end of a period of extra commitment, new leaders need to be continually coming through the ranks of the congregation. Those leaders with the responsibility for the long-term oversight of the congregation need to make sure that, as well as being a worshipping and missionary congregation, they are also a disciple-making congregation. In the next chapter, leadership training as it relates to the local church is examined.

10

DEVELOPING A LOCAL LEADERSHIP TRAINING PROGRAMME

For the first six or seven years of ministry experience, I had one consistent complaint to God, which I often gave vent to in prayer, 'O God, where are some other leaders who can come and help me carry the responsibilities of this work?' It only gradually dawned on me that God didn't plan to send me ready-made leaders. But he was sending me people with leadership potential, and he expected me to provide an environment in which they could grow in maturity, experience and knowledge.

Leaders do not just spontaneously occur, they must be developed consciously. Rob Parsons of CARE for the Family is a very good leader and public speaker who speaks to tens of thousands of people each year. When he was a teenager and a member of a small youth group, the man who led the group told Rob that he had a God-given ability for public speaking. He then offered to help Rob develop his skill. On the first meeting, he set up an old-fashioned flannel-graph and began to tutor Rob on how to speak. From that point on, Rob had the benefit of an older man who was willing to invest time, effort and prayer into a young man with ability. Hindsight reveals that his investment was of immense value.

It is clear that Jesus focused his efforts on the development of leaders. He had just three years to lay the foundations for the church. How many of us would choose his priorities? Church life today indicates that most of us would set about building the largest congregation possible. Jesus aimed primarily for the development of twelve leaders.

The first and most important requirement for the multiplication of leaders to occur must be found in the heart of the existing leadership. The existing leader or leaders must have a deep commitment to investing time, prayer and effort into the lives of emerging leaders. In some cases, they will be more gifted than the leaders who are training them. Rob Parson's tutor was not a famous speaker, but he trained one. Are we willing to invest in those whose ministry will eclipse ours?

That willingness and commitment to train others must be put into action in practical ways, and the action required is always time-consuming. Many leaders never get around to training others because, initially, it is easier and quicker to do the work yourself than to train someone else to do it. Training others does not save time or energy in the short term. In fact, it is both time and energy intensive, but it pays off in the long term.

I was in Christian leadership for eight years before I made the decision to meet regularly and at length with the emerging leaders in my ministry. Up until that time, short-term thinking prevented me from making the best of all investments in the future. I knew the importance of investing in others, but I did not want to set aside the time required for making that investment. From the time I began to take the time and energy required to meet regularly with my emerging leaders, our ministry began to multiply.

The commitment to train others can also be emotionally threatening. Jesus-style training consists of sharing life together. He did not hide himself from his followers. In John 20, he says that a good shepherd knows his sheep and they know him. This statement does not refer to a casual acquaintance, it refers to a deep, intimate knowledge of one another. If we want to multiply effective leaders, we cannot keep others at arm's length, we must be self-revealing. We must be willing to be honest about our struggles, temptations and failings. By being honest, we can develop honesty in others, and that is a pre-requisite for Jesus-style leadership.

There were several powerful national evangelists during the time of John Wesley. Some, like George Whitefield, were more in demand as speakers than Wesley. But Wesley was a man who knew how to train others systematically. He expected honesty and accountability from his leaders and from the people they led. He developed a leadership system of districts and circuits whereby his leaders could cover the nation. Within that system, his leaders met with one another regularly. Wesley developed a series of very personal questions to be used in these small-group meetings, thus assuming that his leaders remained honest and accountable to one another.

We have found some variations of these same questions to be of great value today:

How is your relationship with God? Has he dealt with you about anything this week?

Are your financial matters in good order? Do you have any financial need?

What temptation have you suffered recently and what means of grace did God provide to enable you to resist that temptation?

How is your family life? Is there peace between you and your spouse? Between you and your children?

You can be assured that questions of this nature are a great antidote to boring leadership meetings. As these questions imply, the decision to meet regularly with emerging leaders is only part of the battle. Boring meetings dominated by the pastoral problems of the congregation or by a business agenda will not be conducive to training leaders. The person responsible for leadership meetings must introduce some discipline into the agenda.

Our experience leads us to conclude that there should be three major dimensions to good leadership meetings: Prayer and planning for the ministry we are doing, a business agenda and pastoral care for one another.

Prayer and planning go together quite naturally, as most of the best plans arise out of good prayer times. Many a good evangelistic plan has sprung from prayer for the lost. Plans to plant a new congregation could grow from a prayer meeting about the problem of limited space in your church building. Even after a general plan has been hatched, the details often come together best during or immediately after a good time of prayer.

The business agenda of a leadership meeting is the aspect that requires the most discipline because it can easily expand to take up all available time. There is always more to learn about how to conduct a good business meeting, and books have been written on the subject. We won't go into it in depth here, but we will include a few brief guidelines because a well-run leadership meeting is a great environment for leadership training. There are four broad principles that will improve the quality of business meetings:

1. The senior leader may not be the best person to lead the group through the business agenda. Rotate the leadership and experiment until you find the person most able to keep the business portion of the meeting moving along and on course.
2. Do not deal with matters that can be decided elsewhere.

Too many leadership meetings waste time and energy trying to make decisions that could best be made by an individual or another group. Keep the agenda as small as possible by pushing decisions down to the other groups or individuals.

3. Limit the time available for the business agenda. Before the meeting, decide how much time you will make available to the business, then stick with that decision. If you still find it difficult to keep to a timetable, then think about each agenda item and put individual time limits on them.

4. Advance preparation will help complicated issues move along more quickly. Write down some thoughts and circulate them ahead of the meeting. Or have a smaller group discuss a particularly thorny issue beforehand and then make recommendations to the main meeting.

If this sort of discipline is not imposed on the business agenda, it will inevitably expand to take up all the time available. But by disciplining the business part of a leadership meeting, time can be made available for the prayer and planning that we have already mentioned.

Our experience leads us to conclude that leadership meetings can be most effective for training emerging leaders if they are three-dimensional. We have already mentioned two aspects: Prayer-planning and business. The third dimension takes us back to Wesley's questions: we need an open and honest environment where leaders pastor one another. This can be done by each member of the group answering probing questions like the ones derived from the early Methodists. We have also used an approach that some people have called the 'hot seat'.

In a 'hot seat' session, one of the leaders will take a seat in the centre of the room (with their spouse if possible) and then share anything about which they feel they need prayer. Then all the other members of the group gather around and pray for them. During this time, each of the group should try to be sensitive to the Holy Spirit for any words of encouragement or passages of scripture that might be applicable, or for any God-given insight into the life or circumstances of the person in the 'hot seat'.

These are some of the means by which leaders can be encouraged and trained in the course of normal life and leadership responsibilities. But planned leadership training programmes will greatly increase the number of leaders capable of carrying responsibility in growing congregations. If we take seriously our commission to make disciples of all the world, then we must aim to multiply leaders who can multiply disciples.

It may be that our recent history of church decline has made church leaders fearful of training too many people into leadership – we do not want too many cooks spoiling the broth! Or it may be that the models of church leadership training that have been developed have not released enough of the right kind of leaders to go and pioneer growth in new ground. I recently spent the day with the leadership of one of England's smaller denominations. In this country, this denomination had pursued a policy of not formally training its leaders for several generations, in an attempt to reflect their understanding of the lay-clergy divide. In another part of Europe, the same denomination saw things slightly differently and did have a Bible college. In England the denomination is slowly declining, while in Europe it is one of the fastest growing denominations and is leading the way in church planting.

This is not to say that Bible colleges are the answer to our problems. On the whole, the experience in the UK is that denominations that rely most heavily on colleges to produce their leaders are also the fastest declining. K. S. Latourette, a church historian, has made the observation that over the thousand-year period that the Western Church did not grow either in terms of territory or as a percentage of the world's population, it relied purely on its ordained professional leadership for ministry and missions work. The periods on either side of this hiatus are marked by lay involvement in the Church's mission.

Discipleship can not be left to chance. Deliberate leadership development is essential for the church to engage in ongoing mission, and this cannot all take place in accredited institutions. What is needed is a development of the discipling process that releases more and more church members into a place of active ministry. Just under half of the Gospels' text is made up of Jesus' verbal teaching in the presence of his disciples, and those disciples spent three years living with Jesus and learning by example. Jesus is the Good Shepherd, or perfect pastor, and as it was necessary for him to invest so much of his time into the leadership development of his followers, then every local church leader must in some way carry the same responsibility.

A number of years ago, Youth With A Mission recognized that this discipling process was the biggest single missing factor in the life of the average Western church. Despite being a mission agency the leadership of YWAM felt that they had to plough significant amounts of their resources and time into discipling those young people who came to them, at the expense of the time they would otherwise spend actually doing mission. Subsequently, an international network of Discipleship Training Schools was set up, the idea being that these schools would produce people whose lives would go on bearing fruit wherever they ended up. Today there are literally hundreds of church plants and evangelistic and social action projects that have been initiated and led by 'graduates' of these schools.

Sadly, many found that their newly developed skills, abilities and maturity were at best not appreciated and at worst positively repressed by the churches they returned to. This was due in part to the 'one-man band' model of leadership that has been so prevalent in both the European and American church. We have already stated our position that it is not the job of the local overseer to do all the ministry, but rather to ensure that it is all being done. As the ideas of team ministry have gained ground over recent years, so the number of churches that have seen the need of providing local leadership training has increased.

One such church was Tilehurst Free Church in Reading in Berkshire. In 1986, Bob Smart was invited to join the church as a leader and to help it grow. At that time, it was not strictly a small church, as it had 200 members in a single congregation. Bob had himself just finished the in-house training programme of the Ichthus Christian Fellowship in London and was convinced that the way ahead for the church lay in training more of its members to take on responsible ministry. He persuaded six young people to work alongside him full-time for a year, and Ditchdiggers was born (2 Kings 3:16). Over the next few years, other churches saw the results and the potential of the programme and in 1990 Ditchdiggers was an interchurch venture with thirty trainees working in teams in six church locations.

Teachers on the programme were drawn from all the participating churches, who also underwrote some of the costs; student fees provided the rest. In 1993, Ditchdiggers was restructured to become a part-time course so that more church members could benefit from it. By that time, over 100 full-time students had been trained and over 200 sent on short-term missions overseas; five new churches had been planted; a schools project complete with converted double-decker bus had been established; and Tilehurst Free Church had grown to nearly 400 attenders. The success of Ditchdiggers was at least in part due to the apostolic gifts and abilities of Bob Smart. However, his goals for the church would not have been realizable without this training programme.

Certainly a relationship can be demonstrated around the world between leadership training and growth. In most parts of the world that are experiencing ongoing significant church growth, a programme of training lots of leaders *in situ* can be found. These programmes are sometimes called Theological Training by Extension (or TEE) because the trainee is not just taught how to be a leader, he is also taught how to teach others how to be leaders. Jesus predominantly taught twelve people, but we also find him with seventy-two disciples later on in his ministry. It is not at all unreasonable to assume that the twelve were training the seventy-two; that is, they were training by extension.

TEE programmes are very common in parts of the world that we associate with revival, but this is not purely born out of the necessity for loads of leaders for all the converts. It has often been part of the strategic development that has led to revival. A case in point is India. India contains 16 per cent of the world's population, and 30 per cent of its people groups that have no indigenous church. For years, only 2.6 per cent of the population has been recognized as Christian. This is despite huge missionary resources going into the nation: the organization Every Home for Christ has visited literally every home in the country and delivered a presentation of the gospel in the last thirty years. In the late 1980s, church leaders in India met to consider the challenge of their nation. By the year 2020, India will be the most populous nation on earth, and it has been estimated that by the year 2000 there will be 400,000 rural villages and 600,000 urban colonies with no Christian church. Despite anti-conversion laws in some states, these church leaders set themselves the seemingly impossible goal of planting one million new churches. As a result, groups like Every Home for Christ have changed their approach to evangelism, looking to plant the nucleus of a church in a village rather than visit every home in that village.

One of the most important strategies for reaching this impossible goal is built around a training programme. Under the banner Mission 21 India, a group of denominations and agencies are training twenty church-planting missionaries for each of India's 850 areas of one million people. The graduates of these schools of evangelism then plant churches, train leaders for these churches and train other church planters. Between 1989 and 1991, graduates had planted 18,963 house churches, of which 1772 had not survived. However, it has recently been calculated that each graduate has apprenticed an average of just over twelve new leaders. By 1993, it was estimated that, between them, the graduates and their apprentices had planted over 87,000 new house churches. Most of these have between thirty and sixty members, though some have over 200. By training leaders who could train new leaders, the church in India is perhaps seeing the first breakthrough in growth of the Christian population for many years. Unofficial estimates of the Christian population today put it at 4 per cent.

Of course there is a sense in which many of these programmes can be successful because of the poor education levels of the population generally, as a person does not require a string of letters after their name before their opinion is valued. This is not universally true and it should be noted that even in the educated West there is a shift towards the more intuitive and experiential methods of teaching and training, even in our academic institutions.

Accepting the above limitations, there must be principles involved in TEE which can help shape a local church's discipleship and leadership training.

Whatever form it takes, local leadership training is something that must be happening in a church that wants to be involved in mission, not only because to 'make disciples' requires training, but because experience all over the world confirms that churches that take missions seriously take leadership training seriously. Over the next few pages, we will look at the purpose and philosophy of a local leadership training programme, at a model that can be used to help build a programme, and finally at some of the ways in which such a programme could be implemented by a small local church or a group of churches with limited resources.

THE PURPOSE OF LOCAL LEADERSHIP TRAINING

The purpose of local leadership training must include the objectives of leadership training in general, but also reflect the benefits and disadvantages of its smaller context. In general, leadership training should not simply be looking at accrediting people with qualifications so that they can fill some ecclesiastical position somewhere in the world. It should be looking at nurturing and maturing the ministry gifts required by the Church (apostle, prophet, evangelist, pastor, teacher) and the character and responsibility to steward a local congregation faithfully.

Local leadership training should try to make training available to a wider cross-section of the Church than could take part in a three-year college course. It should also aim to relate the training course to the objectives of the local church's internal structures, its work in the surrounding community and its mission goals.

Finally, in considering the purpose of local leadership training, we need to define what role the programme can realistically play in the development of its participants' leadership potential. In a general sense, a leader is anyone who influences the actions of others, and the process by which someone moves from this general understanding of leadership to a more responsible and recognized one is sometimes called the 'leadership selection process'. Leadership selection is not a one-off experience, it is a process in which God continues to select leaders for more and more demanding roles until they fulfil all that God has for them. This process takes place through a mix of opportunity, training and experience, and while a training programme should aim to provide all three of these, it should also recognize that at best it is only a small part in a long and complex process. When planning local leadership training, we must recognize this reality and then decide what part the training programme can have.

Most churches already have basic discipleship classes, and so we will ignore this aspect of teaching. Barnabas's leadership selection process provides us with a helpful example by which we can gauge what we want to achieve with any programme we develop for our own church. For example, will our programme primarily take committed enthusiasts like Barnabas (Acts 4:36-37) and turn them into people who will take inspired initiative (Acts 9:27)? Will it take initiative takers and prepare them to oversee their own church (Acts 11:22)? Or will it take young church leaders and make them accomplished teachers (Acts 13:1)?

While no programme can guarantee quality leaders who, like Barnabas, will eventually be apostles, it would be good to achieve all three of the above objectives on a regular basis in our churches: to turn enthusiasm into initiative, initiative into responsibility and responsibility into maturity. To achieve these goals, we need to see them as specific purposes of our local training.

THE UNDERLYING PHILOSOPHY OF A LOCAL LEADERSHIP TRAINING PROGRAMME

In all the sorts of training, there are two basic philosophies that govern the development of the training programme. The first is often called the 'traditional schooling philosophy', the second the 'developmental philosophy'. These two philosophies represent the two ends of the spectrum into which all training and teaching fall. The heart of their difference lies in the way in which knowledge is understood, and from this difference flow differing goals and objectives, educational structures and institutions, methods and curricula.

Traditional schooling views knowledge as cognitive – it is purely what you know that counts. There are many many church leaders throughout the world whose qualification for leadership is a piece of paper that confirms that they know the right things, and sadly in many quarters of the church it is not even essential to believe them any more. In its purest form, traditional schooling produces courses for which the primary goal is the accumulation of a body of knowledge by the student and an accreditation. The setting is normally a dedicated building or schoolroom, with an expert teacher giving lectures and setting reading and writing exercises.

On the other hand, the developmental philosophy views knowledge as a mixture of information, skills and experience – learning is about doing and being as well as knowing. From this flows a model of education that puts a higher priority on the development of an individual in his or her gifts than on the attaining of a prescribed level of proficiency A developmental approach leads to training programmes that can take place anywhere, including the classroom. Methods will include practice, reflection and discussion as well as lectures and reading. Teachers are seen as people who are a bit further down the road in a particular skill or knowledge. It is a developmental approach which lies at the heart of the success of so many TEE programmes around the world.

The developmental philosophy has grown in prominence in recent years, with many Bible colleges, like their secular counterparts, moving towards it from the traditional schooling philosophy. However, for many years in the UK it was the close adherence to traditional schooling that distinguished university degrees from those awarded by other colleges. I read an article by a technical journalist recently who was complaining that he had interviewed a number of computer graduates who seemed to know a lot about something, but that it wasn't about computers. His comments were exactly my experience. I took a degree in computer science that prided itself on teaching the abstract principles of the science rather than its current technological state; I then worked in the information technology department of a national bank. One day while at my desk, contemplating the implications of incompatability on the use of symbolic grammars in the development of artificial intelligence, I managed to shut down all the bank's cash-points in the country by not following a simple required procedure. It may be that my error resulted in a blip in the cash flow of the nation which resulted in the subsequent recession causing misery for millions, but I expect it just caused some minor irritation that has gone unrecorded in anybody's memoirs.

However, we cannot be so certain that mistakes made in ministry by freshly graduated but inexperienced Christian leaders, have left such an unmemorable impression on our society. Research carried out in 1994 by *The Times* newspaper showed that England's middle classes were less likely to trust a Christian minister than their children's teachers or the police, and further research in the same year by HarperCollins publishers showed that 79 per cent of the population of the UK still considered itself Christian, but that 77 per cent felt dissatisfied with the Church.

This huge dissatisfaction cannot all be simply a public relations problem. It must in part be due to experience, and any measures that reduce avoidable disappointment should be vigorously pursued. A more developmental approach to leadership training should be able to achieve this by letting trainees make mistakes, which could be pastorally damaging, in a context where the pieces can be picked up by someone else. Certainly, Jesus' training programme was developmental, and when his disciples told the children to 'get lost' Jesus is able to intervene before resentment or disappointment spread through their families. Similarly, when the disciples' inability to help the epileptic boy causes doubt and disappointment in his father, Jesus is able to do something about the father's unbelief (Mark 9:17-27).

A developmental approach to training cannot guarantee that leaders won't make mistakes, however its ability to let someone be a minister while still under supervision must be less conducive to this type of mistake than a traditional schooling approach. If we have to learn by our mistakes, then it is better we do so while we can still reflect on them and receive advice to change our approach or style.

Developmental training is well suited to the local church

and should also be easier to implement at this level than a schooling model, as it does not require vast amounts of expertise before it can be started. Of course, many congregation leaders who will need to be responsible for putting together such training courses will have undergone something more akin to traditional schooling. Therefore, consideration will need to be given to the structure and curriculum to ensure that 'graduates' feel as able to take congregational responsibility as their ordained mentors. For that reason, it is useful to examine a model that has been devised to represent the components of a good developmental training programme and look at how these components could be achieved in the local church.

A GOOD MODEL FOR A LOCAL LEADERSHIP TRAINING PROGRAMME

Over the years, those involved in developmental Christian leadership training have come up with a very good analogy by which to assess their training programmes. The model is called 'Holland's two-track analogy', after its inventor, Dr Fred Holland. The model consists of two train tracks held together by regularly spaced sleepers set in a bed of gravel, and to this basic analogy a number of commentators have made the logical addition of a train. This addition not only allows us to give the model a name with a double meaning, 'train and track', but as we shall see, adds a dynamic to the model which is very important.

The analogy has five components, which represent elements of the structure of a good developmental training programme. The two tracks represent 'input' and 'ministry experience'. The sleepers are regularly spaced periods of 'dynamic reflection', which help relate the input to the experience and make sure that the two are headed in the same direction. The train itself represents the corporate nature of the learning: students should be making progress together as a team and learning the importance of team ministry. Finally, the gravel represents the 'spiritual formation' of the students, the foundation of maturity on which their leadership potential is based.

INPUT AND MINISTRY EXPERIENCE

Educationalists have described three ways in which learning takes place. These are referred to as formal, non-formal and informal. Formal learning refers to learning done within a formal framework, such as lectures, study periods, set reading, etc. Jesus' training programme had many sessions set aside when the disciples would withdraw and be taught in a formal way, the best known of which left us with the Sermon on the Mount. Non-formal learning refers to learning that is organized, but outside the regular programme. Throughout the Gospels we see Jesus using issues highlighted by the flow of events to teach his disciples important lessons. Informal learning refers to learning done in the course of real life; no doubt the disciples did a lot of informal learning on their ministry trips without Jesus.

In the above model, 'input' refers to all formal and most non-formal learning, the structured and planned part of the curriculum that imparts knowledge and skills to the trainee. 'Ministry experience' refers mainly to the informal aspect of learning provided by space planned into the curriculum for skills to be practised and initiative taken in real but monitored situations. Ministry experience provides the ideal setting for informal learning, though a good teacher may take opportunities raised by ministry experiences to give some non-formal instruction on a specific issue. Jesus was exceptionally good at this, using arguments, events and national news to introduce important elements of his teaching agenda. As the model implies, a good training programme maintains a balance between the formal input and real life experience.

The 'train and track' analogy strongly conveys the importance of the experience and input elements of our curriculum progressing in the same direction and at similar speeds. If they do not, the train gets derailed. Biblical teaching and input on preaching techniques need to happen at the same time as opportunities to preach, lead Bible studies and so on. Issues of theology may be better listened to and understood if the trainee has had problems explaining them to an unbeliever whilst evangelizing.

Studies have shown that formal learning is most effective at attaining cognitive goals. Structured classes are likely to be the best way to teach Bible surveys, book outlines and doctrine. Non-formal learning is effective at acquiring the understanding needed to do something. So preaching in the open is more likely to equip someone to do it than a study of 'Paul's open air techniques in the book of Acts'. Regular open-air work will help provide the informal learning that will eventually help turn a trainee into an evangelist.

A good local leadership training programme needs to have fixed periods of formal learning that will cover a predetermined body of material, but it will need to have built into it a flexibility that allows the mentors or teachers to respond to issues and needs as the spirit leads. It must also have plenty of opportunity for real-life ministry, which allows the disciples to learn for themselves their strengths and limitations.

In a local leadership training programme input is likely to

take place in the buildings normally used for Sunday worship or in attached halls; teachers will probably need to be drawn from other local churches and specialist organizations to complement the abilities and experiences of the local ministers. Self-study programmes, tapes and books should not be ignored as ways of supplying specific input that is beyond the experience of local leaders. The exact content of the formal input is likely to vary, depending on the priorities of the leader responsible for putting the course together, although we might expect that it would include some foundational theology, Bible study and evangelism techniques.

Ministry experience should attempt to cover as many areas of church leadership as possible. This will sometimes be in safe, monitored situations – perhaps students will get their first preaching experience by preaching to each other. At other times, experience needs to be real ministry – as when Jesus sends out the seventy-two (Luke 10) with a time of reflection and review at the end of it. As we have already seen, apostles, prophets, evangelists, pastors and teachers tend to draw on the same set of skills, but with varying emphasis and ability. All students should be taught and experience counselling, evangelism, administration, preaching, etc. The particular way in which a trainee's ministry will eventually develop is something that should be determined by the context in which he or she finally ministers.

DYNAMIC REFLECTION

Dynamic reflection is the ongoing process of interactive thinking by which skills and understanding are linked together and become a part of the trainee. Dynamic reflection comes naturally to some, but needs to be encouraged in others. It can be encouraged in a number of ways: one-to-one mentoring with mature members of the congregation, questions and essays built into the formal training, the keeping of personal or team diaries, immediate debriefing after times of ministry and retreats.

Dynamic reflection, like the sleepers of the 'train and track' model, keeps the input and ministry headed in the same direction and imbeds the curriculum into the spiritual formation of the student.

A STRUCTURE TO ENCOURAGE TEAMWORK

As well as teaching the twelve together, Jesus also structured his discipling programme with various sub-teams – Jesus' wider network of seventy-two disciples implies teams of six, led by one of the twelve. When these seventy-two are sent out, they travel in pairs and look for a third person on arrival at a town. Comparisons of the lists of Jesus' twelve disciples implies that it was structured into three teams of four led by Peter, Philip and James.

Though the importance of team ministry is becoming better understood and more desired by church leaders throughout the world, sadly it is still a little realized ideal. While reasons for this are complex, traditional schooling models have tended to encourage one-man leadership by their very structure. Although individual learning is a consequence of traditional schooling, it cannot be assumed that a development model will naturally facilitate team work: it has to be planned in.

A local leadership training programme should have both long-term and short-term teams planned into it. A long-term team may have a particular location assigned over a long period as their evangelism 'patch'. A short-term team may be put together to plan a school holiday club. Over a year, sub-teams of two or three may shadow a church leader for a couple of weeks to be replaced by the next sub-team. Possibilities are endless, but in all ways and at all times a training programme should seek to model and encourage mutual dependency and co-operation.

Teams also give a training programme the ability to let trainees actually be leaders. Within the training context, it may be useful to appoint someone who is naturally a 'number two' to lead a team, as this may be their only opportunity to gain an appreciation of the burdens of ultimate responsibility and could serve them well in the future. Similarly a natural 'number one' may learn some invaluable lessons by serving someone else's agenda for a short while.

SPIRITUAL FORMATION

When describing the purpose of a local leadership training programme earlier in this chapter, its objectives were all presented in terms of its benefit to the church. From the point of view of the individual, spiritual information could be said to be the goal of the course. Spiritual formation is the development of the inner life of an individual so that they experience more of God, exhibit more Christ-like characteristics in their personality and increasingly know the power and presence of God in ministry.

Spiritual formation cannot be taught; it is the goal of the other elements of the course (ministry, input, reflection and team work), and should be the focus of them all. Input can include teaching on Christian character, or it can follow the spiritual formation of a biblical leader. Ministry experience should include planned times of prayer, worship and fasting. Reflection should not just be about how well an event went, but what the trainees gained from organizing it. Team life, perhaps more than any other element, will bring to the surface characteristics in the trainee that need to be changed or healed. In addition, the formation of each student should become a prayer objective of those involved in running the course – individuals could be allocated for prayer to trainers, other trainees or committed congregation members.

The inclusion of spiritual formation in the training model is an attempt to make 'being' goals as important as 'knowing' and 'doing' goals.

PUTTING IT ALL TOGETHER

Putting together a good training programme is time-consuming and resource-intensive, but it is necessary for any church serious about its contribution to the Great Commission. If a church has a couple of hundred members, it may well find it has all the resources it needs within the congregation. This is very unlikely in a church of thirty. It is always important that any training provided locally is relevant to the needs and objectives of the local church. A really small congregation needs to grow, and to do this there may be teaching which the whole congregation would benefit from; this teaching may need to be brought in from outside, or the church may be able to draw on the training resources of its denomination.

Partnership is an ideal way of ensuring that resources are well used. A group of churches may be able to start a training programme, such as Ditchdiggers in Reading, which has already inspired similar courses in several parts of the country. Similarly, specialist training agencies could be approached with a view to providing the input while the local congregation looks after the ministry and pastoral elements of a course. In particular, Youth With A Mission now has an extensive network of people who have led one of their Discipleship Training Schools and who are now beginning to run these courses for local churches. Organizations such as SEAN (Study by Extension for All Nations) produce input materials for TEE and train ministers in how to use them in their churches.

The 'train and track' analogy gives us a model to help us put together the curriculum for a good training programme. In addition, a local organizer has several other considerations. Venue may not be a problem, but does the course require access to library facilities? How will students be recruited? Will it be part time, full time or both? How will it be financed? Does it need to be set up as a charitable trust or separate account? There are multiple solutions to these questions and the many other practicalities that need to be decided before a training programme becomes operational, and it is not envisaged that many training programmes will be started purely on the basis of the material in this chapter. However, we do hope that this chapter will have given some readers a vision for local leadership training along with the basic understanding and confidence to consult further and eventually to start a course that will benefit their own church and the Church at large.

PART FOUR

GETTING IT TOGETHER

11

THE MISSIONARY CONGREGATION

By this stage, some church leaders may be feeling that we are asking them to join a new church network and submit to a modern apostle; run a degree course in church leadership and cross-cultural missions; set up an employment scheme to eradicate poverty in Chipping Somewhere; personally invite one hundred thousand people to a town-wide mission (which they are to organize); and send a third of their sixty members overseas on a long-term mission. With the possible exception of sending a third of their congregation overseas, the above scenario is unlikely to cause the average church leader to leap out of bed on a Monday morning with a spring in their step, a 'hallelujah' on their lips and an eager anticipation of the challenges the new week will throw their way. But all of the principles we have examined and illustrated are capable of being implemented in a church of any size. I know from experience, having been present at the birth of the Ichthus Christian Fellowship, which started with between fourteen and twenty members depending on whether you counted the eight-year-olds like me!

From its inception the Ichthus Christian Fellowship set out to be a church that was three things: an evangelistic local fellowship, a training programme and a mission society. It has always had a team leadership and drawn on outside ministries and resources to help it achieve its vision and fully embody the gospel. Today, the Ichthus Christian Fellowship is made up of about 2000 adults. Its central leadership team now includes some of the ministries who came in from outside agencies to help in the early days. Its training programme is much more complex in structure and is being exported to other parts of the country. And as a mission agency, Ichthus has built up an expertise that allowed it to become the first local church in the UK to become a member of the Evangelical Missionary Alliance.

While the shape, size and structure of the Ichthus Christian Fellowship today does not bear much resemblance to the average small local church, all of its current ministry is built on principles pioneered while the church was less than one hundred strong. As we start to try to fit the pieces together to build a missionary congregation, it will be helpful to review the ways in which Ichthus went about training, evangelizing, missioning and fellowshipping while it was still small, and then to think about the possibilities open to the imaginary Downour Street Independent Church as it moves from a maintenance to a missions mode.

FELLOWSHIP

At the heart of a missionary congregation must be a community of people who love each other. If there isn't, then the church's wider ministry of reconciliation is undermined. The development of a good fellowship life was not seen as distinct from Ichthus's other aims: mission and training. Fellowship was the embodiment of the gospel to be preached and the fruit of the discipleship and training. While the church was small, maintaining the quality of fellowship was relatively easy. Growth made it possible to come to the meetings without the commitment to the people and vision of the church. As the church has grown, it has tried out a number of cell meeting structures, events and church holidays to foster deeper relationships. Even today, a large part of the church all go away together each year for a week of camping.

The quality of fellowship is something that the small group should find easier than the larger group, even though many small churches still seem to fail to achieve it. This may in part be due to the different reasons members of the congregation have for attending.

Being a new church gave Ichthus an advantage that has been recognized by many church planters since: to some degree, all of the original members shared the same vision and expectations for their new church. Where a church has even a few years of history, its aim and vision can become unclear. When the vision becomes unclear in a church, people will attend and join for reasons that relate more to their own individual pleasure and comfort than to a purpose. Almost by definition their motives will be selfish.

I was speaking recently with one couple in the fellowship who confessed that by preference, in terms of worship style and church structure, they were Anglicans, but they shared the Ichthus commitment to mission and evangelism. This commitment to a common vision overrode all other considerations and preferences.

Research seems to indicate that nearly two thirds of all Protestant churches in the UK have no mission vision or mission statement. But fellowship that is built around a purpose seems to be more robust, durable and deeper than fellowship that is built in natural friendships and tolerance. Many smaller congregations would find their fellowship enhanced if they could adopt an understanding of who they are, based on their missions context. If they could discern the purposes for which God has called them into existence, the members will be less likely to evaluate the congregation from a selfish perspective. In addition to this pragmatic factor, it is biblically far more common to find a church recognized by its missions context than by some factor related to the style or status of its members.

As well as having a clear understanding of why they existed as a church, the early members of Ichthus took on a commitment to build quality into their corporate life. This commitment was expressed in three ideals or resolutions which the founding members adopted:

1. To love one another. This commitment held the team together through some difficult times and was openly taught to the rest of the congregation.
2. To esteem humility. The church would stay open to ideas from outside and not assume that they knew how they were going to achieve everything they were setting out to do.
3. To stay open to the Holy Spirit in all areas of church life and structure. In theory, all churches would say that they were open to the Holy Spirit's guidance. But very often so little changes that we must assume that the church has failed to hear the gentle urgings of the Spirit.

As Ichthus has grown, so has the detail and scope of its mission statement. The process of redefining and focusing a mission statement acts as a continuing opportunity for members to reaffirm their commitment to the church's aims and objectives, and therefore to each other. Over the years, there has been a continual change in the structures of Ichthus and a development of its theology. For many, this has made Ichthus an uncomfortable church to be a part of and it is an ongoing joke that even the leaders have to go to the newcomers' meetings to keep up with the latest developments!

MISSION

Written into the Ichthus Christian Fellowship's Trust Deed is the fact that mission is a major part of the purpose of the fellowship. As a reflection of this commitment, a substantial part of the budget (in excess of a quarter each year) is given to evangelism and overseas work. A few years ago, the church was investigated by the Inland Revenue who could not believe that the church was giving as much as it was overseas for legitimate reasons. Needless to say, their investigation concluded that everything was above board.

In their immediate context, Ichthus has always had a policy of presenting a full gospel of words, works and wonders. Wonders cannot always be planned for, but those involved in evangelism have always been taught to pray with expectancy for all contacts and friends, and as a result a number of people have been healed and subsequently given their lives to Jesus. These have included a great variety of people: those from other faiths, atheists, drug users, the clinically depressed, old and young alike. There have also been those who have been healed and yet who have not become Christians.

To represent the church's social concern locally, they started a programme, which they called Jesus Action, to serve needs in the community. In its early days it was organized very informally, being little more than a title to represent the church's social concern to the local authority and the community at large. Church members simply made their time and skills available for referrals from the social services or from evangelism contacts. Early on, Jesus Action developed ways of passing on second-hand furniture, children's clothes and so on to those who needed them. Acts of service such as regularly shopping for an elderly person or mowing a disabled person's lawn were often given to non-

Christian teenagers who had been reached through the church's youth outreach. Several of those teenagers became Ichthus's first converts, and today a number of them are involved in full-time Christian ministry.

As the church has grown and developed, the social concern embodied by Jesus Action has given rise to distinct projects, such as a crisis pregnancy counselling clinic, a launderette to act as a community focus on one estate, a credit union, a life skills course and a primary school. Although each of these initiatives has become a self-supporting project in its own right, they have all been born out of the church's loosely structured social concern which still operates under the title Jesus Action. Many small churches could benefit from simply giving their social concern a title, drawing up a list of members' skills, willingness and availability for service and advertising their presence to local community groups.

Even when it was a very small church, evangelism went hand-in-hand with Ichthus's social action programme. Ichthus was fortunate in having a very evangelistically minded leadership team – this was the reason they had come together in the first place. In Chapter 9 we commented that, while this is highly desirable, it is not the norm. Leading by example, the original leadership team was able to inspire every member of the church, from the youngest to the oldest, to be involved in open-air and door-to-door work. While pressures on time have meant that the leadership team can no longer do so much evangelism themselves, there is still a commitment to lead by example. One trainee evangelist was quite awe-struck by the fact she had spent the morning doing door-to-door work with the church's founding pastor, Roger Forster, and the afternoon doing door-to-door work with its worship leader, Graham Kendrick.

Accepting that only 35 per cent of churches seem to have any sort of evangelism leader, (see Chapter 9), there are still things which a pastor or teacher can do to lead the congregation in evangelism. The research by the Evangelical Alliance already quoted found that 85 per cent of church leaders encouraged their congregations to share their faith, but 29 per cent of leaders spent less than 5 per cent of their time in evangelism, and 49 per cent spent less than 10 per cent of their time in this way. In the same vein, over 60 per cent of the ministers who could answer said that less than 10 per cent of their leadership planning meetings were taken up with logical evangelism issues. The same survey found 77 per cent of the ministers polled felt that they had to provide all of the pastoral attention asked for by their congregations.

These statistics seem to confirm that we usually give ourselves to the activities we are most comfortable with. Not many pastoral leaders find it easy to set aside the time for evangelism, but every congregation needs to see their leaders taking a lead in evangelism. Undoubtedly, an extra hour or two a week could be put into evangelistic activities without depriving the people of pastoral care. A church leader who does not feel that she or he is a natural evangelist would set their congregation a wonderful example if they committed a regular amount of time to making new contacts with the community.

In addition to their commitment to be 'good news' to their immediate context, the Ichthus Christian Fellowship has always been involved in overseas mission. In the early days this was achieved by partnerships with agencies and societies that had more expertise than the local congregation. Through these partnerships, the church gradually built up its own resource of skills, often by drawing people into the congregation who had served with the agencies they were working with. These people would in turn bring an emphasis, knowledge and enthusiasm for mission that infected the rest of the church.

Even before the Ichthus Christian Fellowship had started, Roger Forster had taken the initiative to visit the churches in a number of Eastern bloc countries to offer support and teaching. While on these trips he would smuggle in Christian literature, Bibles and teaching materials on audio tape. When he first started there were no special agencies to help with this work, but he would find a Christian who spoke the language and they would make contacts and build up plans from scratch. When Ichthus was started, the congregation followed his example, with many members participating in such trips. In fact, one of the first converts was arrested and interrogated by the KGB for smuggling Bibles into the Soviet Union.

One of the first people to become a member of Ichthus was an elderly Christian who had committed herself to pray for a missionary in Turkey. Roger Forster was able to meet this missionary on a ministry trip and, through this contact, a relationship was developed which resulted in the church developing a special interest in Turkey. The missionary and his family eventually moved to work with Ichthus, reaching Turks in London and creating a relational bridge for extensive outreach and church planting in Turkey.

By divine providence rather than considered planning, Ichthus discovered two principles that are of benefit to any local church that wants to get involved in missions work. The first is that congregation members actually need to go out on the mission field, not just be told about it or send money to it. Their experience becomes part of the whole church's experience and a general confidence and expertise is nurtured in the home church.

Second, focusing on a particular project, place or people

involves the congregation far more emotionally and solicits a greater commitment than simply supporting a mission society or agency. It also enables the congregation to develop expertise in their particular part of the Great Commission, thus becoming a resource to others in the future. Ichthus's involvement with Turkey has given it an active role in the translation and distribution of a modern Turkish Bible, and the church's missions department is often consulted by missionary agencies working in Turkey. The church also helps train Korean missionaries on their way to Turkey each year.

Today, there are multitudinous opportunities for local churches with limited resources to get directly involved in missions in almost any part of the world. There are information centres collecting data on every group of people and nation in the world to be used by churches that want to take an active role in reaching a particular place or people. There are agencies offering short-term experience or evangelism holidays as well as traditional vocational training and placement. However, the two principles – broad involvement of the congregation in all sorts of missions experience with all sorts of other agencies in all sorts of places, and the specific targeting of the church's main focus onto a particular place, project or people – are still likely to be relevant to the developing missionary congregation.

DISCIPLESHIP AND LEADERSHIP TRAINING

By 1993, training in Ichthus was highly organized, modularized and comprehensive in its coverage, offering modules in New Testament Greek and church history as well as prophecy and counselling, and experience in evangelism and overseas mission work. But it began small, and it has maintained continuity with the training provided within the church in the early years in that it is still on-the-job training and tied to ministry experience.

In many ways Ichthus' training programme was an extension of its discipleship programme. All new converts went through a basic discipleship course. At the end of it, those who wanted to go on as Christians were offered a mentor to work with them 'one to one'. In addition, someone who had just completed a discipleship course would be asked to co-lead the next course. This basic approach of training people to train others is at the heart of all fruitful church training programmes. As the process continues, trainees are prepared for even more responsibility and new input has to be designed to provide further training as the whole body grows.

Ichthus also started to take on individuals from elsewhere to train in evangelism. These were often recruited through university Christian Union meetings or ministry in other churches by Ichthus leaders. In all of these training situations, trainees were growing in knowledge, skills and maturity and at the same time the church was benefiting from their energy and ministry.

Eventually the one and twos became fives and sixes and a more organized year-long training programme, called Network, was developed. Network eventually developed to be able to cater for more than thirty students a year, and graduates from the programmes have planted other churches in the UK, France, Denmark, Central Asia and elsewhere. They lead churches of all kinds of denominations, they work with many different mission agencies and some have even stayed on to help lead and work with Ichthus.

For the small church, the immediate implications of

taking on the training of new leaders are the same as for becoming more evangelistic. It is the time the local leader makes available to the pastoral needs of the congregation that will need to be eaten into. Being a mentor to one or two trainees need not cost the church a huge amount, but it will take up the pastor's time in the short term for the possibility of returns in the long term.

In reviewing the way in which the Ichthus Christian Fellowship implemented many of the ideas we have presented in this book in their early days, we must remember that many things have changed in the last twenty years. Research into the world's less reached regions has opened all sorts of new doors for local churches; less formal courses and teaching materials have been developed by a number of organizations and new and creative methodologies have been tried and tested. To help the local church move into a missionary future we need to think about the current possibilities as well as the successes of the past. To do that we will use the hypothetical Downour Street Independent Church.

DOWNOUR STREET INDEPENDENT CHURCH

Downour Street Independent Church, an imaginary church, has sixty-five regular adult members and twenty-seven children. Its meeting hall is on a main road a couple of miles out of Typicalton town centre. The church is led by Joe Pastor who has a team of two other elders; in addition, a member of the congregation makes an invaluable contribution by leading worship and the church's prayer programme. After bills and pastor's salary, Downour Street regularly has £5000 of disposable income a year. Some of this money is used to make gifts to various Christian charities, another portion is used for special evangelistic services during the year (visiting speaker, drama group's leaflets, etc), some is set aside for future building work on the 100-year old hall and a portion is saved for a regular five-yearly mission which Downour Street helps organize with a couple of similar churches in other parts of the town. Downour Street, like 49 per cent of Protestant churches, spends less than 5 per cent of its budget on local evangelism.

Joe Pastor is a member of the local 'Churches Together in Typicalton' ministers fraternal and at recent meetings, he has been impressed by the contributions of one of the other ministers. His church has been changing considerably as he has followed the lead of others in his denomination and sought to develop a missionary congregation. After much prayer and reflection and discussion with his elders and other mature members of the congregation, Joe has decided that this is the right direction for his church too.

His first problem is that the church doesn't have an evangelism leader. All of Joe's role models for Christian leadership were pastors, all his training was to equip him to be a pastor and Bible teacher. One of the elders, Bill, has recently taken early retirement. While he wouldn't consider himself an evangelist, he does now have the time to develop new evangelistic ideas and lead the church in them. The budget is trimmed to give Bill £3500 of the church's disposable income (between 5 per cent and 10 per cent of the total church budget), to develop and implement a long-term evangelistic strategy and tactics for the church. Bill is publicly recognized as the church's evangelism leader.

The other elder, Ben, has been responsible for the church's overseas missions giving for several years now, and it seems sensible for him to be given the responsibility for instilling a more active participation in overseas missions within the congregation.

Also in the congregation is a new university graduate, Steve, who while at college had led several friends to the Lord and had spent most of his summer holidays working with various evangelistic agencies. He would love to spend a year working and training with an evangelistic agency. Joe agrees that over the next six months he will help Steve raise some support from members of the congregation while Steve saves some of his own money. The church members are asked to support Steve for two years, and during the course of the second year, Steve will work for the church on probation while they assess whether they can afford or should take him on as a full-time or part-time evangelistic worker. During the second year, Joe will act as a mentor to Steve who will be set a study programme under Joe's supervision.

Meanwhile Bill has attended a conference which helped him to realize that the skills acquired in years of marketing can be adapted to help him (and the congregation) better to understand the social environment surrounding the church. The church is situated in an area bounded by a railway line, a canal and a main road, and although the 15,000 plus people who live in the area are socially and racially mixed, these physical barriers do create some sense of community, which is reflected by the fact that most of the congregation lives within this triangle.

Bill is delighted to have discovered a starting point for fulfilling his evangelism brief and enthusiastically organizes the church to survey the area. Bill adapts a questionnaire which asks such questions as whether people consider themselves part of any religion, and if so do they attend a place of worship and where is it. The object of the exercise is not to be evangelistic in itself, rather it is to gather information for future planning, and to give congregation members a way to get to know some neighbours without feeling too threatened.

The research shows the church that a larger number of people still regard themselves as Christian than the church had suspected. It also shows them that there is a small but significant group of Muslims in the area. Bill's analysis of the results also reveals that those who never attend church also very rarely have Christian friends. Based on this information, Bill decides to break his thinking and planning into three areas. Most of the congregation should feel confident in reaching the lapsed Christians, a smaller more skilled and motivated group would need to take on the challenge of developing a means to reach the non-Christians, and outside help is likely to be needed to reach the Muslim section of the community.

Research done at the local library brings further light to Bill's task. Data from the UN census shows that most of the South Asians in the area live in just five streets. In addition, Bill discovered that council housing policy has filled one small estate right next to the church with single-parent families. The church's questionnaire confirms that this is an area in which few people worship anywhere. The church has two single mums in the congregation, one of whom lives on the estate, and her contacts could provide a starting point for reaching this area of need. Bill also finds out that over 40 per cent of the households in this area have no access to a car, and this figure rises to over 65 per cent in some streets and estates. Bill realizes that their strategy must be based on 'we go to them', rather than 'they come to us'.

While Bill has been conducting his research, Joe has visited the five other churches in the area. One church has a 'gathering' philosophy, drawing people from a wide area for a particular theology and style of worship and they seem to have no interest in the surrounding community. The Anglican church has a very large parish which includes Downour Street, but the focus of their own evangelistic activity is elsewhere. Another church refuses to meet with Joe, but the last two churches share Downour Street's concern for the area. The three churches agree to keep each other informed about plans and activities and, where possible, to support each other's projects.

Ben has noted that Bill's research has discovered some local Bangladeshis. Part of Downour's mission giving goes to a missionary in Bangladesh, and Ben realizes that, if their giving comes from a genuine concern to reach Bangladeshis, then they must find a way to reach members of this very same people group who live in their town. Within a few weeks, Ben shares his thoughts at the church prayer meeting and a new conviction is born amongst the members: their involvement with Bangladesh must become more informed and more personal, so they resolve to find out all they can about Bangladesh and its people.

After some general enquiries to agencies listed in the UK Christian Handbook (which he persuades his local library to buy), Ben gets three replies which move him further towards the church's new cross-cultural missions programme. One is from a company that runs a 'travel agency', who offer to organize a tour of Bangladesh and recommend that the church send a party of six or more on a 'holiday with a purpose'. The second reply is from the Alliance of Asian Christians in Britain, who offered to put the church in contact with any Christians from the areas that the church might develop an interest in. The third is a referral to a North American missions research centre that has up-to-date information on Christian mission and activity in Bangladesh. If the church has access to a computer with a modem, they can get regular prayer information sent to them about the peoples of Bangladesh and the needs of missionaries working there. A teacher in the congregation does have access to a compatible computer at school and is able to join an international computer network for less than £8 a month and the cost of a local phone call. Now the church can receive current and specific news and prayer requests, a vast improvement on the vague information which used to be posted on their missionary bulletin board.

Ben liaises with Lydia, the woman who leads worship and prayer at Downour Street, to make sure that the regular information gets to the midweek prayer meetings and to the small but growing number of committed intercessors. Lydia senses that all this new missionary and evangelistic activity could be just the thing to revitalize the church's prayer life, so she starts to think about an integrated prayer strategy to undergird all this new activity. First, she makes a public request for people in the congregation who will commit themselves to pray for at least one half-hour period a week for the church and its work. She, for her part, will provide a weekly prayer update for the intercessors. And the church answerphone will be used to take general prayer requests from the congregation which will be passed on to the people committed to pray for the church and its work.

She also talks to Joe and Bill and starts to put together a 'spiritual map' of the area. She marks out areas of need – like the estate of single parents uncovered by Bill's research, and the South Asian community, and another area of quite expensive houses where the survey found no people who attended church regularly. She uses different coloured pins to signify the homes of Downour Street's members and the members of the other co-operating churches. Finally she gets hold of a copy of the electoral register for the area. Each week, her prayer information includes two or three pertinent facts about a particular segment of the area. She also lists about seventy families on the electoral register by name. In this way, nearly every family will be prayed for by name every two years.

As a result of the church's new promotion of local evangelism and an interest in Bangladesh, one mum realizes that she has often spoken to a couple of Bangladeshi mums outside her children's school. She makes a personal commitment to develop this contact into genuine friendship if at all possible.

Bill's research has given him some ideas for a local evangelism strategy. The large number of single mums on the estate next to the church are a section of the community with obvious needs that the church could help meet with only a small amount of new effort. Bill persuades the parents that run the church's 'mums and toddlers' group to become the heart of a new 'parent support club'. The mums and toddlers group is made up of church mums and their friends, and so far, no special effort has been made to bring in mothers from the estate. Bill gets teenagers in the church to sign up to a cheap baby-sitting service list, gets permission to use some of the church hall's roof storage to store second-hand children's clothes and toys and starts collecting these items from church members. He applies for a grant from the local council to provide new equipment for the newly formed club. The church also decides to open up the Sunday school to children whose parents don't go to the church. This provides a child-minding service on Sunday mornings and parents coming to collect their children often stop to have coffee with the rest of the congregation.

The new 'parent support club' is advertised by a handbill to every home on the estate and one of the single mums in the church is given as a contact name and address. She also actively uses her own relationships to recruit members, and all of this results in a growing contact with single parents on the estate. The club, the used-clothing bank and the reasonably priced pool of baby-sitters proves to 'scratch people where they itch', and many new friendships form, out of which there is a steady trickle of conversions and new church members.

For the more general population, Lydia's map and electoral roll inspire Bill to develop a door-to-door strategy with the other two evangelistic churches in the area. Between them they produce a small pack, which contains information about the three churches and imminent special events, a presentation of the gospel for adults and for children, a leaflet containing testimonies by three local people, a freepost response card and details of a help-request phone number that one of the other churches agrees to set up. Each week, leaders and members from the three churches address and personally deliver the packs to the homes being prayed for by Lydia's intercessors. Packs are always delivered personally and the recipients told that the area is being prayed for and that prayer requests are welcome.

Within this comprehensive programme of visitation, the three churches plan a series of special services, events and youth activities. The three churches also decide specifically to target lapsed members and nominal Christians. They collect resources and ideas from a number of resource agencies and plan a series of invitation events. They then build an invitation list with names drawn from old Sunday school records and church member lists, plus the non-church-attenders in Bill's survey who called themselves Christians and who said they were happy to receive further information from the church. In addition, Bill discovers a marketing company that has been asking questions about church attendance and religious affiliation in their lifestyle questionnaire. From this company, Bill buys a mailing list of everyone in Typicalton who said they were Christians but who didn't regularly attend church. The list has over 300 names on it.

For Joe, with his pastor's heart, all of this activity has brought a pleasant surprise. Each of the new programmes involve a handful of his members, thus giving them an outlet for service, and he notices that pastoral crises and needs actually seem to be declining amongst those active members. The new converts, however, more than replace the reduced counselling roll. Those new converts are much more prepared than his original core of members to share their needs and difficulties with someone other than the senior pastor, and this gives him an opportunity to act as mentor to some of his original members in whom he recognizes a shepherd's heart, but who had no previous outlet.

But as the church takes on more projects and initiatives, they need to see new leaders emerging with other areas of expertise, areas outside Joe's experience. After talking to the other two co-operating churches, Joe contacts a number of agencies and arranges a year-long series of monthly lectures and workshops. The teaching includes a 'Perspectives on World Missions' course taught by a group from Youth With A Mission, a Bible overview taught by someone from Walk Thru' the Bible and open-air preaching techniques taught by someone from Campus Crusade for Christ. Joe provides input on how to study the Bible, pastoral care and other subjects he feels confident in. Links are formed with a large multi-congregational church in a nearby town who help provide teaching on subjects where they have more experience. Participants are organized into evaluation groups, in which they keep check of each other's spiritual growth and present Bible studies of their own. Joe invites five mature members of the congregation to lead these evaluation groups and gives them further personal input himself.

In the autumn, Joe, Ben and four other church members take a 'holiday' in Bangladesh. Before going they arrange to meet up with some Christian workers whose details they obtain via their computer link with the North American agency. The group returns with a new enthusiasm for the area and the Christians they have met. They start an aid fund which will be directly related to the projects they have developed relationships with. So that the fund doesn't drain too much of the church's resources, Bill suggests that raising finances for it could be a good means of making further contact with the community.

The teacher who has been collecting information about the region on the school computer organizes some project work and sponsored events at his school, and some of the disillusioned Christians contacted through the church's work with their fringe are asked if they would like to use some of their professional skills and time to support this fund and raise finances. Finally, leaders of the local Bangladeshi community are asked if they would be able to advise this openly Christian fund on the way it allocates its funds.

One year on from Joe's decision to try and be more of a missionary congregation, the leadership team, which has grown to include Lydia and Bob (one of the evaluation group leaders) draws together their experiences and formulates out a vision statement for the church which includes their commitment to bring in God's kingdom in the immediate area, in the whole town and in their part of Bangladesh. They then write a succinct prayer and get it printed on bookmarks and simple posters for all church members. Bob then gets the prayer printed onto some coffee mugs as he reasons that most people drink more cups of coffee in a day than they have Bible studies.

On Steve's return from his year of training, the leadership team decide that he ought to establish some schools work in the area and also look into leading a small team from the new training programme in starting a satellite congregation or house group. Another pioneer house group is planned for the next-door estate, building on contacts made by the 'Parent Support Club' and also using a team from the training programme. A third team from the training pro-gramme is taking a special interest in the nearby Bangla-deshi community, and a contact from the Alliance of Asian Christians is giving them special instruction on cultural topics and overseeing their attempts at learning the language together using a tape learning system.

Over the year, the link between the three Typicalton churches and the large church in the next town have developed and a prayer retreat is organized for leaders from the four churches. Some of the leaders of this larger church become regular visitors to the Typicalton churches, and their input is often inspirational and their presence starts to convey to the congregations that they are part of something big and exciting. The main pastor of the large church is very interested in Downour Street's developing overseas programme and gets Joe invited to speak at a number of leaders' conferences. At these conferences, Joe finds himself continually exposed to new ideas and ministries and finds that his own thinking about his church's missionary role is sharpened.

Downour Street has no guarantee that all their initiatives will lead to growth and success. In fact, as every pastor knows, there will be some major disappointments along the way. Perhaps Steve, after all the church's investment in him, will suddenly announce that he is leaving the church to take up an attractive job offer in another part of the country. Joe and the leadership team might be even tempted to decide that all these initiatives are more trouble than they are worth. But the creative use of their resources and co-operation with other local churches and national and international organizations has meant that a small increase in commitment and giving has sown the seeds for growth, a clearer identity for the church and a much greater sense of purpose and significance. Downour Street is now more definitely a 'church' in the best sense of the word - a congregation of people on the move.

Of course, it is all very easy to make it happen in an imaginary church. But we hope that Downour Street is not so far removed from most churches and, therefore, that many will be able to draw some ideas and inspirations from it.

In more general terms we may summarize the way in which a church will develop its missionary activity into three phases; people, position, prayer and policy.

PEOPLE

People are the foundation of almost everything the Lord does. The first step in building a missionary congregation is to recognize the people who have particular interests and encourage them to start taking initiative. While they may not be given a title (titles given too soon can certainly cause problems), every church needs to have a someone to take responsibility for the church's local evangelism, its social concern, its overseas involvement and its discipleship and training work. These people need to be relatively mature Christians, though not necessarily ready for full overseer-style responsibility. They will probably need others around them with the same interests and vision to form *ad hoc* action groups.

It is in these groups that a church will find the enthusiasm, time and energy to develop new ideas and initiatives. In time, action groups will acquire a level of expertise which is not possible if everyone in the church is responsible for all aspects of the church's ministry.

POSITION

Eventually, if a church is to be fully involved in mission, it will need to start drawing the leaders and some members of the action groups into recognized positions of leadership. Without the recognition of the work being done and the lead being taken by the *ad hoc* action groups, their work will never become a part of the congregation's life. Rather, it will tend to be viewed as an added extra for those who feel so inclined. The action groups need to be given the power to contribute to any changes to the church's structure and programme.

As well as the leadership recognition, the whole congregation needs to be drawn into the work and ideas of these groups, perhaps through input at Sunday services or inclusion in the church's prayer life.

PRAYER

Many project failures, pastoral problems and potential church schisms can be avoided if good ideas for new initiatives are first brought to the church in prayer. When a body of believers meets to pray, discuss, and then pray some more, this often provides an ideal environment for the people to feel a growing ownership of the ideas being presented. On the other hand, many good ideas do not prove to be in God's plan for that particular congregation. And it is much less painful to discern that in prayer first, rather than to reach the same conclusion some months later after the expenditure of much time, effort and money.

In addition to the way prayer can play a key part in the practical outworking of good leadership, it also opens the door to the dynamic supernatural dimension which is meant to be part of all church life. Virtually everyone reading this book will agree with that statement, but they will also be aware of the need to live more consistently with their beliefs on the subject of prayer. The experience of many church leaders is that the prayer meetings are the least attended events in the church calendar. Perhaps the most common reason for this is that prayer meetings are too rarely tied into dynamic vision and decision-making for the direction of the church.

POLICY

If an action group's idea and plans are ever to come to fruition, it will need finances. Each action group will need some control of a portion of the church's budget. If it is true that where our treasure is, there our heart is, then it would seem that giving to these areas of ministry will actually help the congregation develop a heart for the work. It will usually also increase the congregation's giving.

Of course, with finances comes accountability. Each action group ought to formulate some statement of vision, policy and budget for the church's leaders to refine and approve and for the whole church to adopt. This helps clarify the congregation's commitment and keeps the action group focused.

A FINAL CHECKLIST

Putting all this together, we can create a straightforward checklist for the aspiring missionary congregation. For each of the areas of ministry mentioned above – evangelism, overseas mission, social concern, and training – the church leadership must ask: do we have reasonably responsible and mature people with a natural interest? (Remember that at the outset, they will rarely seem to be as responsible and mature as we would like). Are there others who could join with them to start an *ad hoc* action group? Does the church recognize people in leadership for these four areas of ministry and are they free to initiate change within the appropriate procedures? Does the church have a statement of policy for each of these areas of ministry and does it have a budget for them? When people are the missing link in the chain, we need to ask ourselves, 'Is there an outside agency which might help meet the need?'

THE FAITH FACTOR

Finally, we must remember that faith should be foundational to all we do as a church. Unfortunately the visions and aspirations of many congregations don't inspire much faith or even require much faith to achieve. In this book, we have sought to present a big vision for the small church. It is a vision that requires faith. In Heb 11, we read that without faith it is impossible to please God. The authors are fully aware that the job of turning a congregation inside-out is not an easy job. To do so will require church leaders to have the convictions of things only previously hoped for (Heb 11:1). But if that is not the case, then we won't be pleasing the Lord. The building of thousands of missionary congregations, if done in the right spirit, will be a wonderful act of worship because it will stretch and increase our faith. And as John Wesley once wrote, 'faith laughs at the impossibilities and cries, "it shall be done." '

BIBLIOGRAPHY

Jesus and Gospel Tradition by C. K. Barrett, SPCK.

UK Christian Handbook Edited by Peter Brierley, Christian Research Organization.

Church Planting at the End of the 20th Century by Charles Chaney.

'Unique Dynamics of a Small Church', a paper by Carl Dudley.

Cinderella with Amnesia by Michael Griffiths, Intervarsity.

Operation World: Handbook for World Intercession by Patrick Johnson, Send the Light.

Understanding Church Growth by Donald McGavran, Eerdmans.

DAWN 2000: 7,000,000 Churches To Go by Jim Montgomery, Highland.

The Community of the King by Howard Snyder.

HANDBOOKS OF PASTORAL CARE

General Editor: Marlene Cohen

This series is an aid for all involved in the pastoral ministry. Informed by biblical theology, the series offers practical resources for counselling while emphasizing the importance of a wider context of care in which the Christian community, prayer, preaching and nurture are essential to wellbeing and growth. Details of the first volumes are given on the following pages.

Handbooks of Pastoral Care Series

GROWING THROUGH
LOSS AND GRIEF

Althea Pearson

All of life involves loss. Whether great or small, reactions to loss frequently follow a common pattern. From even minor experiences of loss, counsellors can gain valuable insights into major traumas such as redundancy, sexual abuse, marriage failure, declining health or bereavement.

From her extensive experience as a counsellor and trainer, Dr Althea Pearson also demonstrates that loss, however traumatic, always brings some measure of gain in its wake. Therefore, though tackling a subject which requires the greatest sensitivity on the part of the counsellor, *Growing Through Loss and Grief* helps to show the way to new understandings, fresh hopes and new beginnings.

FREE TO LOVE
Margaret Gill

Sexuality lies at the heart of our deepest human needs for companionship, intimacy and acceptance, yet through fear, ignorance and emotional hurts, it is often regarded as a sleeping snake, best left untouched. Many counsellors and pastoral carers are not sufficiently at ease with their own sexuality to help those experiencing sexual difficulties to the place of healing and freedom to which a full recognition of the God-givenness of sexuality can lead.

Free To Love brings together Margaret Gill's extensive experience as a medical doctor working in psychosexual medicine and as a Christian counsellor. Her deeply sensitive, wise and professional approach will be an invaluable guide to all aspects of sexual identity and experience encountered in pastoral care today.

FAMILY COUNSELLING
John and Olive Drane

The Christian Church's lofty teaching on family life all too often imposes unrealistic ideals, which tend to magnify the normal stresses felt by any family. A sense of guilt for failing to achieve perceived Christian standards often compounds other problems. When those problems are serious, denial is commonplace and yet another family is well on the way to being screwed-up.

John and Olive Drane first question the evangelical definition of a family, looking beyond the Western nuclear family for a better model. Biblical characters who are often held up as shining examples are honestly appraised, and the stereotypic advice sometimes given by clergy is brought under critical review.

Sweeping these unhelpful, burdensome attitudes aside, the authors suggest a more realistic and compassionate way that the Church can affirm and support families.

John Drane is Director of the Centre for Christian Spirituality and Contemporary Society at the University of Stirling. The place of the family in the Church has long been a concern of John and his wife Olive, and they have co-authored several published articles on the subject.

FOR BETTER, FOR WORSE
Mary and Bruce Reddrop

An extremely wise, sensitive and informed guide for Christian counselling dealing with marriage problems. Emphasis is given to the counsellors' own categories of thinking, Christian belief about marriage, appropriate and inappropriate psychological strategies, etc., with the goal of increasing counsellors' competence and self-understanding. Practical chapters deal with identifying root problems and their origins, biblical anthropology (and its various interpretations), the nature of marital breakdown, feelings and behaviour, causes of conflict, sexual difficulties, separation and divorce, counselling for change, and much more.

The Reddrops are a highly experienced team. Mary trained as a teacher and social worker and was Director of Family Life Education for the Marriage Guidance Council of Victoria before establishing her own private practice as a psychotherapist. She is also supervisor and trainer for the Anglican Marriage Guidance Council in Melbourne, of which her husband, Bruce, was Director for almost thirty years. He is also Founding President of the Australian Association of Marriage and Family Counsellors.